Oboe Reed Styles

Oboe Reed Styles

THEORY AND PRACTICE

DAVID A. LEDET

Foreword by Richard Killmer

INDIANA UNIVERSITY PRESS

Bloomington and Indianapolis

This book is a publication of

Indiana University Press
601 North Morton Street
Bloomington, IN 47404-3797 USA

http://iupress.indiana.edu

Telephone orders   800-842-6796
Fax orders   812-855-7931
Orders by e-mail   iuporder@indiana.edu

The paper used in this publication meets the minimum requirements
of American National Standard for Information Sciences—Permanence
of Paper for Printed Library Materials, ANSI Z39.48-1984.

Manufactured in the United States of America

The Library of Congress has cataloged the hardcover edition as follows:

Ledet, David.
    Oboe reed styles.
    Bibliography: p.
    1. Oboe—Reeds. I. Title.
ML941.L4   788'.72   80-8152
ISBN 0-253-37891-5

ISBN 978-0-253-21392-1 (pbk.)

2   3   4   5   13   12   11

"Some Men, I must confess, endeavour to Decry the Hautboy, pretending the Learners must blow so hard, that it is apt to bloat their Faces, and prejudice their Lungs: But this is a meer Mistake, as will be found on Experience: For all that play upon this Instrument, to a reasonable perfection, know, That with a good Reed it goes as easie and as soft as the Flute."

> J. B. [John Banister II?],
> *The Sprightly Companion . . .*
> *Plain and Easy Directions for*
> *Playing on the Hautboy*

"The reed, properly speaking, is the heart of the oboe."

> Garnier, l'aîné [François
> Joseph], *Méthode Raisonée*
> *Pour le Haut-bois . . .*

CONTENTS

PART I: TONE PRODUCTION

PART II: OBOE REEDS

List of Tables

Foreword

RICHARD KILLMER

UPON MY ARRIVAL at the Eastman School of Music in the fall of 1982 I had a wonderful meeting with my predecessor Robert Sprenkle (1914–1988). Among many topics discussed was a thorough and incredible study done by oboist David Ledet, who had produced a two-volume Ph.D. thesis dealing with the oboe and the reed. (I had met Dr. Ledet in Denver, Colorado, in the early 1960s, when he performed as oboe soloist with the Community Arts Symphony of Englewood, Colorado.) This exhaustive work included an oboe reed "how to" section which was, in 1961, published as a part of the Robert Sprenkle/David Ledet book *The Art of Oboe Playing.* In addition to that portion of the thesis were an explanation of the basics of oboe tone production and other important pedagogical issues, and an amazing series of pictures of oboe reeds, collected over a period of many years. Although the thesis was completed in 1960, it was not until 1981 that part 1 (Tone Production) and part 2 (Oboe Reeds) were published as *Oboe Reed Styles: Theory and Practice.* During 1979–1980 Dr. Ledet "upgraded" the earlier material prior to its 1981 publication.

As with any "picture book" it is simply easy to look through without reading the printed word. And since the pictures were so compelling I spent a great deal of time there, perusing the marvelous and varied examples of oboe reeds. Some were made by oboists with whom I was familiar, including my own teacher Robert Bloom, but many were made by artists unknown to me. The "reed insight" contained here was remarkable: various reed lengths, scrape lengths, and tip design among other attributes.

During the twenty-six years I have been teaching oboe at the Eastman School of Music I have shared these examples with countless students as we met the challenges of making reeds. From time to time we would even consult the tables in the back to consider the range of possibilities with regard to issues such as gouge thickness, shaper size, tie length, and tip dimensions. However, what I have found equally compelling are the biographical sketches and "point-of-view" comments from both the participants and the author. Here is where we can better understand what an oboist is thinking as he or she makes their reeds. Many of the persons whose information and reeds are contained in this volume are no longer with us, making this documentation invaluable as a history of the oboe reed during the first half of the twentieth century. This was certainly a formative time in oboe playing and oboe reed pedagogy. There are several excellent books on reed-making, each of which present a singular system for making the reed, but this book offers the "worldwide" range of reed styles.

Today there are at least a dozen gouging machines available for purchase as well as at least two dozen shaper tips, many of which were designed only recently. The gradual evolution of both gouging machines and shaper tips has brought about a greater standard and consistency of reed-making. The distribution of general reed-making knowledge is now quite widespread. This is due to the fine teachers of today who are diligent in discovering better ways of making reeds and teaching reed-making, and the teachers of the past, who, without the sophisticated technology of today, were, nevertheless, able to produce wonderful music on the oboe.

In spite of these improvements in the equipment used in making reeds as well as the increased knowledge of our craft, this book is as pertinent today as it was when first written and published. It continues to be an important source of information. Even with the technological advances, much about oboe playing remains the same. We are all striving to make music on the oboe, enabled by our reeds rather than being disabled by them. The International Double Reed Society has brought countless oboists together, both in the publications and the yearly conventions. Whether at an IDRS convention, a private lesson, a Master Class, or even in a rehearsal, oboists from around the world ask, "How do you make your reeds?"

Acknowledgments

THE WRITER WISHES to express his gratitude to Dr. Donald Smith, Research Chemist, Eastman Kodak Company, and Mr. Henry Hulett, Art Department, University of Georgia, whose technical knowledge and encouragement made the photographs possible. The writer is also indebted to the many artist-oboists throughout the world who contributed so willingly in time and effort to this project.

On the personal side, the writer wishes to acknowledge his wife, Marlene Ledet; Mr. Robert Sprenkle; and Mr. Marcel Tabuteau for their unselfish assistance.

Introduction

FROM THE STANDPOINT of both the teacher and the student, reed-making is one of the most important aspects in the pedagogy of the oboe. The making of reeds by the oboist is an inseparable part of his learning to play the instrument successfully. There are several principal reasons why reedmaking and successful oboe playing are so closely related:

1. An oboist's style of playing is dictated in large part by his choice of reed. Articulation, breathing, flexibility, and intonation are affected by the particular reed.
2. The oboist's aural conception of sound—his ideal tone quality—is successfully achieved to a great degree by his choice of reed.
3. Variation of quality and pitch in oboes makes it necessary for the student to make a reed that will complement his particular instrument.
4. Physical characteristics of players temper the tonal results. Thus, an individualized reed becomes imperative for the person who wishes to be more than a mediocre performer.
5. Because of the impermanent nature of reeds, the oboist must constantly replenish his supply.
6. Commercial reeds are generally inadequate. They seldom, if ever, suit to the fullest extent the individual needs of the player. They merely serve the purpose of supplying something for a beginner to use, inadequate as it may be, until he can make his own reeds.

The writer finds that one of the best approaches to better teaching and playing of the oboe is through the presentation, delineation, and interpretation of the styles of oboe reedmaking as related to tone production. *How* and *why* oboe reeds sound as they do can very well be explained through the several schools, or styles, of reedmaking that have evolved. In Part I of this work, factors pertinent to the production of tone on the oboe are discussed in separate chapters as an aid to understanding fully why oboe reed styles exist and what these styles are. Respiration, articulation, embouchure, instrument, acoustics, and the effect of the listener on the player influence overall reed styles as well as the minute alterations of the reed that an artist-performer makes in order to achieve a certain timbre or response. When one sees an oboist remove the reed from the oboe and carefully make a few strokes of the knife on certain parts of the reed, he is observing an age-old operation. The oboist is exercising his ability to suit the reed more to his method of tone production and playing needs. These few strokes usually represent the considered judgment of the player and are the culmination of a rather complex system of thought, action, and reaction based upon the desires of the player and the laws of cause and effect as those laws apply to reedmaking.

The player's method of tone production—the way he breathes, his style of articulation, the type and use of his embouchure, etc. —will affect the timbre and response of the reed and will, consequently, affect its measurements and, therefore, its visual form. A player's composite method of tone production can come about as the result of his having been taught a particular way, by his individual experimentation, or by a compromise between the two. However, in the end, the player tries to achieve a complementary balance between his methods of tone production, reed, instrument, listener, music, and playing situation whereby he can play with the greatest amount of efficiency and satisfaction. This work deals, therefore, with the elements of tone production as *links in the chain* of factors contributing to reed styles.

It has long been recognized by oboists that certain reed styles exist, but views and terminology conflict, as in many other inadequately documented fields. A logical approach to the problem of delineating reed styles is through an investigation of the actual reeds of recognized artists and reedmakers. Part II of this book is a photographic and statistical presentation of reeds of individual oboists, with short autobiographies and remarks by the players about their reeds. Eighty-two selected artist-players from 14 countries have provided a total of 168 examples of reeds. A study of the collective examples provides a rather broad basis for judging the current styles of and possibilities for reedmaking. Through the survey to date the writer has been able to set apart 5 definite styles of oboe reeds and 1 borderline style. By examining the visual and dimensional representations of the styles of reed these artist-players make, one can appraise his own reeds on an international scale.

The conclusion can be drawn that the cut of a player's reed is dependent upon the method of tone production (way of breathing, use of embrochure, etc.), the instrument, the teacher (or teachers), and the aural concept of the player. On the one hand, the cut of a player's reed will dictate in large part the amount of control he will get in tone quality, articulation, dynamics, etc. On the other hand, the amount of control the player desires in tone quality, articulation, dynamics, etc., will dictate the cut of the reed. It is evident from the photographs and measurements of individual reeds in Part II that seldom are the reeds of one player like those of another. Indeed, even separate reeds made by a single player are often quite disparate in appearance and measurement, but, of course, all reeds do have certain common characteristics.

Heretofore, measurements and photographic representations of oboe reeds from throughout the Western world have not been made. Most of our information on this subject has been gathered by word of mouth, from teacher to student, or through a few precious periodical articles by oboists who have travelled and reported their findings. The measurements and photographs of the reeds in chapters 7 and 9 provide an account of just what the limitations and possibilities are in this field at the present time. The measurements are useful because they account for many of the reasons why and how a reed sounds as it does. The comparative proportions of a reed can be used as guideposts to achieving a particular type of sound.

Unfortunately, a work of this nature cannot do one thing. It cannot express the aural sensation of a reed style or of the reeds of the individual oboists represented. The inadequacy of words to express a timbre is well known; nothing can duplicate the actual sound of these players in their playing situation. However, phonograph recordings of many of these players are available and some are so noted. An excellent source of information, international in scope, regarding available phonograph recordings of oboists is the current yearly Artist Issue of the Schwann Catalogue[1] available at most record stores in the United States. Players are listed according to instrument and also by their orchestras, trios, quartets, etc. The scientific measurement of aural concept (psychoacoustics) is not within the province of this book; consequently, the aural concepts of these reeds, whenever stated, are those of the writer and a number of colleagues and, of course, lie within the area of subjective sensation. However, the scientific approach through measurement and visual representation has been used and is desirable as far as it can take us. If we cannot reproduce the sound, we can measure and photograph, an alternative that gives us at least that much of a description of the reeds and, in reality, perhaps a more objective analysis after all.

Many of the fundamental principles of reedmaking are the same, regardless of the particular school of playing. All aspiring reedmakers must learn to use certain materials and learn certain introductory operations. For example, it is necessary for all reedmakers to learn to use a knife, plaque, and mandrel; to learn about shape and gouge of cane; and to learn a method of binding the cane on the staple. Consequently, in the chapter on reed styles and in the photographs, the reader will note that all players must work with the same materials, but through the process of variation and refinement they suit their own necessities and concepts. These variations and refinements are manifested in measurements, visual forms, and ultimately in timbres and musical control factors.

What is best? This is a question that cannot be answered. What is best for one may not be for another. We can only *state the outside limitations of the present acoustical system that is in use by artist-players*. In the matter of reeds, the reader will note many similarities, but also many differences. However, it would be a serious error to cease asking, "What is best?" Perhaps another way, validly considered and properly investigated, would be better for a given individual.

To an oboist, reeds are exciting things, being as they are the very essence of the timbre and technique that are so important to musical performance. A particular style of reed is an index to a certain timbre and technique of playing. To reiterate, by a realistic appraisal of the various styles of reeds and their resultant possibilities for tone and control, a player can exercise an intelligent selection and adjustment of his reeds and thereby improve his performing ability.

PART ONE

Tone Production

1

Respiration

THE OBOIST'S METHOD of tone production has a great influence on the type of reed he will use. In Part I, intended as background material to the later discussion of reeds themselves, the writer will examine in sequence all the other links in the chain of tone production: respiration, the open throat, articulation, embouchure, the instrument, the acoustics of the room, and the listener. These factors will all be related to timbre, technique, and pedagogy, which, in turn, influence reed styles.

This chapter deals with one of the most important links in the chain of tone production, because respiration and breath support are the very foundations of oboe playing. All players do not use the same breathing technique. Some may use the lower ribs more advantageously than others, or use the slowly moving fix (fig. 4), or have a more or less constricted throat. Some players may naturally blow more vigorously than others. These differences of breathing technique contribute, through the principle of chain reaction (breathing technique affects the throat, embouchure, fingers, etc.), to *why* and *how* an oboist cuts his reed the way he does, and thereby influence reed styles. The following discussion will set forth which muscles contribute substantially to the breathing process by being tense, which ones contribute by nonopposition, and just how much air pressure is required for efficient play-ing. Most of this matter of respiration is approached from an analytical and pedagogical standpoint.

THE MUSCLES INVOLVED
IN RESPIRATION[1]

One single muscle—the diaphragm—and two sets of muscles—the abdominal muscles and those of the thoracic cavity—are more im-portant to correct respiration than any other muscles of the body.

The *diaphragm* is probably the most important muscle used in breathing. It is a large, thin, dome-shaped muscle, which is joined at the sternum or breast bone and around the diameter of the tho-racic cavity in the area of the lower six ribs on either side. It is joined in the back by two tendons, which attach to the upper three lumbar vertebrae, and it separates the thoracic cavity from the abdominal viscera. The central tendon comprises the highest part of the dome and actually supplies much of the tension that causes the diaphragm to contract. The diaphragm is much higher in the body than is usually imagined, the top of the dome lying higher than the point of the breast bone. One very important thing about the action of the diaphragm is that *when it contracts, it pulls downward.* However, in its most violent contraction it moves downward only about 30 millimeters. Consequently, *it is primarily a muscle of inspiration. It has absolutely no ability to move itself upward.* It can move upward only through relaxation of the dia-phragm itself, or it may be pushed up through a chain reaction started by the tensing of the abdominal or other muscles. What many musicians think to be diaphragm movement is actually the displaced abdominal viscera moving to the front. For our pur-poses, the abdominal viscera (under the diaphragm) can be thought of as a large plastic bag of water, which cannot be appre-ciably compressed, but can be displaced. When the central tendon of the diaphragm pulls down upon the top of the abdominal vis-cera, the viscera are displaced transversely and to the front. The abdominal walls are elastic when the abdominal muscles are not being contracted against them; therefore, the displaced viscera push the region of the "stomach" outward. The distance the diaphragm moves downward, of its own volition, varies with the posture of the subject. It moves farthest when a person is lying supine, a position that minimizes resistance to the diaphragm's contraction. When a person stands, the normal movement downward is less, and it becomes smallest when a person is in a sitting position. This information would lead us to believe, and rightly so, that it is actually easier to breathe, either naturally or forcefully, when one is lying on his back. Oboists, of course, do not normally play the oboe in this position. Therefore, we may surmise that among the positions normally available to oboists, it is easier to breathe naturally, deeply, or forcefully, while standing rather than while sitting.

Now, because the diaphragm can only move downward and is therefore most useful only in inhaling, there are other muscles that must aid in forceful exhaling. The important *abdominal muscles* used in playing the oboe are the Oblique externus, Oblique internus, Transversus, Rectus, and Pyramidalis. The first three lie in three layers a bit to either side of the center line of the abdomen. The Rectii are long muscles that run down the center from the sternum to well below the navel and are perhaps the most important of this group for exhalation and for the production of vibrato. The Pyramidalis is called into action when more violent respiration is executed.

The important inspirational *muscles of the thorax* are the diaphragm, Intercostales externi, Intercostales interni, Serratus posterior inferior, Serratus posterior superior, Subcostals, Transversus thoracis, and the Levatores costarum. The first four are the most important. The last four are usually used through mutual action and interaction and in more violent respiration.

The diaphragm was discussed above because of its singular importance. The intercostal muscles are two thin planes of muscular and tendinous fibers occupying each of the spaces between the ribs. Named *external* and *internal* from their surface relations, the external intercostals act to raise the ribs in inspiration while the internal intercostals act to lower the ribs in expiration. Though the elevating inspiratory action of the external intercostals is admitted by nearly all authors, the function of the internal intercostals has been much disputed. Some observers deny that either set of intercostal muscles takes any part in raising or lowering the ribs.

One other muscle group of the thoracic region should be singled

out as being fairly important—the Serratus posterior inferior.
These muscles originate, four on either side of the spinal column,
in the area of the eleventh and twelfth thoracic vertebrae and the
first and second sacral vertebrae. They flow upward from their
juncture with the spinal column and join to the back sides of the
ninth, tenth, eleventh, and twelfth ribs on either side. These are
the muscles that elevate or expand the lower ribs.

It should be noted that when the term *costal muscles* is used, it
refers not to any one specific muscle but to all the muscles affect-
ing the ribs. It is derived from *costae*, or ribs.

The *lungs* fill most of the area within the rib cage, branching to
the right and left at the termination of the trachea. The area between the lungs, over the center of the diaphragm, and behind the
sternum, is occupied by the heart. The lungs' importance in general respiration is, of course, obvious. In the production of oboe
tone, they are important because they govern the vital capacity
of air and they also form the sac or bellows from which air is
expelled, ultimately to vibrate the reed. Their expansion and contraction cause the rib cage to rise and fall slightly. *The lungs are
not muscular, but they are elastic.* If expanded, they tend to return
to a smaller size. Thus they do somewhat aid the support of the
air column by virtue of this elasticity, after the downward contraction of the diaphragm has released its influence.

According to one authority, there are 52 paired muscles of the
thorax, 8 paired of the abdomen and pelvis, 16 paired of the neck,
and 112 paired of the back. A great number of these muscles are
employed in breathing, but they are not used voluntarily, i.e., because we *will* them to be used. They are used involuntarily as reciprocal muscles to the main ones discussed above and as muscle
groups that learn to work together or move as the result of a more
basic muscle movement.

There is considerable physical movement for each cycle of respiration. Most of it is unseen and should *not* be consciously felt.
For example, for every inspiration there are over 94 joints in the
rib cage alone that move. Many of the muscle and joint movements are only slight, and some muscles are not used at all except in
violent respiration.

Many anatomy and physiology books distinguish between quiet

or ordinary breathing and deep, extraordinary, or violent breathing. For playing the oboe, we breathe a bit more than just quietly, but not violently. The *amount of muscular control used* and the *muscles from which this control comes* are paramount factors in the correct expiration of breath. We try to use only those muscles which are necessary in order to breathe as simply and efficiently as possible. This can be accomplished with conscious use of the relatively few muscles that have been described above. The next sections will deal with the actual use of these muscles in the production of oboe tone.

THE MECHANICS OF RESPIRATION

There are several so-called systems of breathing for playing the oboe. All of them, of course, make use of the expiration of air to vibrate the reed. Therefore, there is only one way to breathe, the physiological way, which simply involves *inspiration* (inhalation) and *expiration* (exhalation). Together they constitute *respiration.* The differences inherent in systems of breathing then lie in the various *uses* of the muscles involved in respiration. The way regarded as superior by most authorities can best be described as being executed predominately by the diaphragm and the abdominal muscles (mainly the Rectii). This method works out in practice to aid rather than inhibit tone quality, tonguing, and endurance. It is actually the most natural and uncomplicated process.

First of all, the player's posture should be conducive to good respiration. If the player is sitting, his head should be kept up with the chin extended neither up nor down. Lowering the head can lead to bringing the shoulders forward, which tends to constrict the upper chest and cuts down the total potential capacity of the lungs by an amazingly high percentage. The shoulders should be comfortably back and the spinal column straight. No indication of the familiar "slump" should be present in the posture. The body should be bent forward slightly at the hips and relaxed. If there is a bit of tension felt after the passage of time, it should be only in those muscles which support the spinal column and keep the upper part of the body from collapsing completely. The balance should be such that a person could rise to his feet at any time.

It would be hard to overemphasize the importance of good posture. Not only does it aid in mental alertness but also it puts the
body, if properly relaxed, into a position whereby the breathing
muscles can operate in their most efficient manner.

INSPIRATION

For inspiration one inhales through the mouth and at the same
time expands the lower ribs. At the outset of the inspiration, the
diaphragm will contract and move downward (fig. 1). Allow the
lungs to expand in all their diameters, with particular attention to
the bottom portions. As the diaphragm is contracted, more air is
drawn into the lungs. The rib cage is expanded *naturally* (that is,
it is not opposed by the costal muscles) as a result of (1) the enlarging lungs and (2) the diaphragm's reaching its downward limit
and pressing against the resistance of the abdominal wall. Note that
the abdominal muscles are always relaxed for inspiration.

The diaphragm reaches its downward limit quite soon. As has

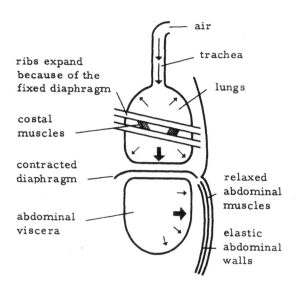

FIG. 1 Inspiration. Normal or forceful.
Read from top.

been mentioned, in the most violent breathing the diaphragm contracts downward only about 30 millimeters. The central tendon, the top of the dome of the diaphragm, applied to the abdominal viscera, then becomes a fixed point for the action of the diaphragm, the effect of which is to elevate the lower ribs and, through them, to push forward the body of the breast bone and the upper ribs. This is what we call expansion of the rib cage.

As the diaphragm is drawn downward, it pushes the abdominal viscera before it, and because of the elastic abdominal walls and relaxed abdominal muscles, the "stomach" region swells or bulges. This is a desirable feeling and appearance. We usually take in our full capacity of air without straining. This air should normally be taken through the mouth, but there are times in playing when it is advantageous to inhale through the nose.

EXPIRATION

When the oboist exhales to play, he should use the normal, quiet, involuntary expiration process, which the body does natu-

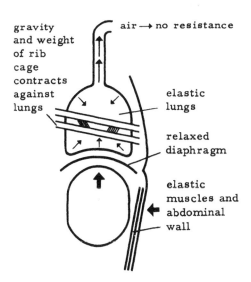

Fig. 2 Normal quiet expiration. Read up.

rally (fig. 2), but he should also add the use of the abdominal muscles, primarily the Rectii. Consequently, expiration for the oboist
could best be described as forceful expiration or perhaps even
breath support. The Rectii should contract and give enough pressure or support to push the air up and through the reed. A reed
with a small opening and little resistance requires less muscular
support than a stiff reed (and the two reeds will sound and sometimes look different from each other). At the end of the inhalation
process, there is an instant when the air is compressed behind the
tongue, giving the necessary amount of support from the beginning of the tone to stabilize the sound. This principle is discussed
at greater length in the following section on articulation.

In correct forceful expiration, as in figure 3, the air moves upward and outward as the result of the pulling inward of the abdominal muscles and the elasticity of the abdominal walls, diaphragm, lungs, and rib cage. The abdominal muscles push against
the abdominal viscera, which, in turn, push upward against the
relaxed diaphragm. The diaphragm moves upward of its own
accord, because of its relaxation, and transmits energy upward to
the lungs. The lungs are elastic and will, therefore, aid expiration
of their own accord, as does the diaphragm. The foregoing chain
of events moves the air upward and outward. The air should move
upward preferably through a relaxed throat; the air column should
not be inhibited by the glottis. The lower ribs usually are kept
reasonably expanded when exhaling. There should be a slight natural falling of the breast bone and rib cage, but the costal muscles
should be passive.

In the production of oboe tone, the relaxed diaphragm of figure
3 is more desirable than the "slowly moving muscular fix" of figure 4, because the *difference* between the pressures exerted by the
two opposing forces in figure 3 (in this case, the diaphragm and
the abdominal muscles) will do the same amount of work as is
accomplished in figure 4. For example, if the abdominal muscles
were exerting 1 pound of pressure against an opposing .5 pounds
of pressure from the diaphragm, as in figure 4, .5 pounds would be
effective at the reed. This method is a way to control the amount
of air pressure at the reed, and many instrumentalists use this type
of controlled breathing. But in this type, opposing forces will,

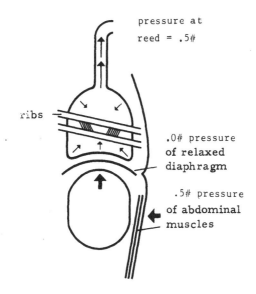

pressure at
reed = .5#

ribs

.0# pressure
of relaxed
diaphragm

.5# pressure
of abdominal
muscles

FIG. 3 Correct forceful expiration. Read up.

over a period of time, lead to tenseness and fatigue. Now, on the other hand, if we wish, or need, .5 pounds of pressure at the reed (fig. 3), we simply apply .5 pounds' pressure with the abdominal muscles against *o pounds* of opposition from the diaphragm and the same amount of pressure at the reed is gained (.5 pounds) with less tenseness and ultimate fatigue. For playing the oboe, the latter method is far superior.

The question is asked many times, "Just how hard should one blow to play the oboe?" The answer is that *the force from the abdominal muscles should be just strong enough to balance the resistance of the reed and to stabilize the pitch, response, timbre, and intensity of the tone.* This concept places great emphasis squarely upon the amount of resistance in the reed. If the reed is stiff, it will take greater air velocity (dependent upon greater pressure) to cause it to vibrate. This factor then places a greater strain on the embouchure to keep it from simply "blowing out." One of the functions of the embouchure is to keep the compressed air

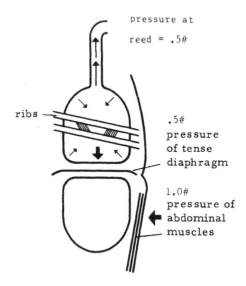

FIG. 4 Forceful expiration. The slowly moving fix.
Read up.

(compressed between the abdominal muscles and the resistance of
the reed) from leaking out from around the sides of the reed. The
more pressure the embouchure has to work against, either to keep
air from leaking or to control the reed, the less endurance it will
have because of muscular fatigue. We should understand that the
abdominal muscles are stronger than the lip muscles. Blowing
against too much resistance will sooner or later, depending upon
the amount of resistance in the reed, only cause the abdominal
muscles to overcome or fatigue the lip muscles. When this happens, the player is, of course, incapacitated as far as artistic playing is concerned, because he simply has less control of the reed
with his weakened embouchure. Only rest will alleviate this state.

How much resistance should there be in a reed? There should
be an adequate amount for the player to perform efficiently. By
"efficiently" we mean to be able to play artistically that oboe literature which makes reasonable physical demands on the player.

Many symphony oboists play and practice only the rather short and limited excerpts that they must perform in the orchestra, forsaking much of the rich literature of the instrument. They can, therefore, play on heavier reeds, with which it would be very difficult to play a major solo work. They also allow themselves the rather dubious luxury of playing on heavier reeds at times in order to "sound darker." However, if faced with having to play the étude, concerto, and sonata literature, or the solo oboe parts of Bach cantatas, they find that they suddenly do not have the necessary breath control or embouchure endurance. This method may be expeditious for the job at hand, but it is certainly not efficient playing in the sense of being able to play well enough at all times to handle the literature of the instrument.

Sometimes after a layoff, a student will prefer a reed with more resistance. He feels more secure with the greater resistance because of a less sensitive, weaker embouchure. This is actually a false feeling of security, because he is merely adding more responsibility to an already weakened embouchure, without getting the fineness of control that he desires. Also, after a layoff, other playing faults such as tight throat, tense fingers, and unequal embouchure tend to be exaggerated.

It has been the writer's experience that sometimes one can play with less effort than he thinks he can. As has been stated, a little less resistance sometimes can make playing possible over greater lengths of time with greater musical control. An adjustment can be made many times in reed style, embouchure, or instrument to make up for the less resistance.

The foregoing discussion is to point out that there must be a delicate balance between the elements of the breathing apparatus, the embouchure, and the reed resistance. One can "bully" an embouchure just so much with heavy reeds and faulty breathing habits before losing that fine control so necessary to artistic playing. But when the balance is such that one feels the mutual, reciprocal interplay of the correct air pressure against correct resistance, the vibrato works well, the throat tends to relax, the tongue is freer, the ebb and flow of dynamic range is comfortable, one may "open up" to project the sound, and, above all, the embouchure is not overpowered. The embouchure can then do its job without fighting the great odds of too much air pressure, a large reed opening, and too much resistance in the reed. Consequently, the amount of air pressure that the player habitually uses to vibrate the reed greatly influences the scrape of the reed and vice versa.

In our discussion of breathing and reed resistance, there has been considerable mention of *less* resistance. How little resistance can be tolerated? There is not enough resistance in the reed if the player cannot feel the "core" or "center" in the reed. Too little resistance in a reed tends toward a sound that is too "light" in weight and color.[2]

How much air pressure does it take to vibrate a given reed? This is dependent in part upon the resistance in the reed, but the writer finds that when he plays on reeds that he normally makes, the mean air pressure (measured by a simple manometer) varies from about 5 to 7 ounces. This is, of course, an individual matter and varies within reason, as it should, between players. Now—and this is an important point—this mean air pressure, causing the air to pass through the reed with a certain velocity, *may or may not vary* with support from the abdominal muscles. It is possible, as we have seen in the concept of the slowly moving muscular fix, to support very much indeed without actually raising the air pressure at the opening of the reed (see fig. 4). This is done by *tightening* the abdominal muscles *against* a *contracting* diaphragm and then allowing the downward pressure of the diaphragm to be overcome by the inward-upward pressure of the abdominal muscles, which results in a certain air pressure at the opening of the reed. If the pressures of the two opposing forces are equal, then there is no air movement upward from the lungs and into the mouth. If the downward pressure of the diaphragm is allowed to be *more* overcome by the inward-upward pressure of the abdominal muscles, then the air in the mouth comes under higher pressure (against the reed) because it is not protected as much by the diaphragm from the superior force of the abdominal muscles. Conversely, if the downward pressure of the diaphragm is allowed to overcome a relaxing inward-upward pressure of the abdominal muscles, the air pressure at the reed falls.

There is also the interesting opposite phenomenon, in which

one may concentrate on keeping the air pressure *constant* (above, we thought of the pressure in the mouth rising or falling as the fix moves). One moves this muscular fix (the abdominal muscles against the diaphragm) up and down by allowing either one to overcome the other *without changing the air pressure*. This is possible simply because the *total* fix is moving upward. The movement of the two opposing muscular elements is simply a subdivision of the total fix. If this were not true, no air would move up from the lungs—the breathing condition would be static.

As was pointed out at the beginning of this discussion, the technique of breathing correctly is extremely important, because it is the very foundation upon which the other contributing factors of tone production are built. The following section deals with the next step in the chain of tone production.

THE OPEN THROAT

Another contributing factor to good tone production, and therefore an influence on reed styles, is the degree of constriction in the player's throat. The concept of the open throat in relation to producing a tone on the oboe can hardly be overemphasized. The muscles that tighten the throat and close the glottis should be relaxed. If the throat is constricted or the glottis partially closed, many of the benefits of correct breathing can be lost. A simple way to check for a tight throat is to ask the student to say "oouu" and play a note on the oboe simultaneously. In the writer's experience more students cannot do this on the first trial than can. Of those who cannot do it on the first trial, some pick it up readily within the first half-dozen tries, while others have trouble relaxing the necessary muscles and need help. For those who have difficulty, we find that "sneaking up on the reed" is a workable solution. The student is asked to blow out his breath against some resistance of pursed lips, then to say "oouu" and do the same thing. When he can do this and direct a reasonably forceful stream of air through his lips, the reed (in the oboe) is placed in the opening of the embouchure and blown through a few times (not vibrating the reed). Next he should blow, say "oouu," gradually tighten the embouchure around the reed, and listen for the air going through the reed. When sufficient air speed and embouchure firmness are reached, the reed will start to vibrate. At times the student will get to the point of vibrating the reed, but the "oouu" will stop. After a few trials, he is usually successful in keeping both the sound and the tone going at the same time. It is helpful to the student if the instructor will continually ask, "How does it *feel* to blow that way?" By building a mental image of the "feel" or "sensation" of the action, the student, through repetition, will be able to learn the technique. At first the tone will be wild, but soon the student will learn to contract the muscles of the embouchure without tightening the muscles of the throat. There will be a very noticeable swelling of the outside diameter of the neck and a greater use of the abdominal muscles. It should be emphasized again and again that the "feeling" for correct blowing while actually playing is the same as saying "oouu" and blowing at the same time, and that even when the vowel sound is stopped, the feeling in the throat and the abdominal muscles should remain the same. One should feel as if the vocal cords could be activated at any time while he is blowing. Some teachers tell their students to "hum" and blow at the same time. This is not exactly what is wanted because humming necessitates the vocal sound's coming through the nose, considerably higher and more forward than the "oouu" in the throat. The writer condones either as a desirable pedagogical technique but considers it undesirable practice to do either when playing in public because of the unmusical extraneous noise associated with the techniques, especially if it can be heard by the audience. It is possible to allow air to escape through the nose while playing, but in this instance we do not want a true hum. Saying "oouu" puts the air through the mouth, where it should be for this little test. After a few weeks of practice with this conception of breathing and open throat, the student realizes that there is *no muscular tension except at the abdominal muscles and at the embouchure.* All other muscles in between are passive. The importance of the constant attention to the feel or sensation of this open throat lies in the fact that the student may very well understand everything the teacher tells him, but if he does not knowingly experience it, he does not fully realize the sensation.

THE EFFECT OF CORRECT RESPIRATION
AND THE OPEN THROAT ON
TIMBRE, EMBOUCHURE, AND REEDS

There are certain beneficial results that can come from using the proper methods of tone production: (1) the tone should be bigger, more resonant, and more freely produced; (2) intonation should be improved; (3) longer phrases and more expressive playing with a properly produced vibrato will be possible; (4) a full breath can be taken in an instant; (5) the player will have more embouchure endurance; (6) reeds can be balanced to a finer point by minute alterations of the scrape.

In the preceding paragraphs we have considered a method of breathing that *aids* rather than *inhibits* the playing of the oboe. The primary raw materials of playing that have been discussed thus far are muscles and air. The most important concepts regarding the use of these raw materials are (1) that air can and should be under pressure and (2) that only certain muscles can and should be willfully put under tension. The aim has been to set forth which muscles contribute most by being tense, which ones contribute by nonopposition, and just how much air pressure is required. All of these considerations lead to one end—to give the performer an efficient basic technique of playing so that he will not be hindered but, on the contrary, may progress to the limit of his abilities and play with as much musical control as his inherent or learned sense of artistry will allow him to play. As we shall see later, this state can lead to variations of reed style.

HOW TO TEACH CORRECT
RESPIRATION

There is only one way to learn to breathe correctly for playing the oboe, namely, by actually *doing* it and observing the aural and physical results. This is a significant concept, because there are many students and teachers (coaches) who mentally understand and feel capable of criticizing an action, but who have no idea how it "feels" to do it.

Breathing is primarily a muscular function and thereby subject

somewhat to the will. With a little practice, it is possible to isolate
and move separately the important breathing muscles, i.e., the diaphragm, the abdominal muscles, the intercostals, and the Serratus
posterior inferior. Actually, a great deal of the many other muscles used in breathing are not used and cannot be used entirely
voluntarily. It is not advisable to try to use these muscles voluntarily. Many come into use as the result of sympathetic or reciprocal innervation. In other words, they work together to arrive at
the end result.

Basically, the writer teaches breathing in the following steps:

1. The correct pattern is coached by first giving the student an
understanding of the desired physical movements and by getting
him to play a tone demonstrating his concept of good breathing.

2. Since "feel" develops with practice, repetition should be encouraged. As the desired movements and their visual and *tonal*
results improve through practice and analysis, the statement should
be constantly made to the student, "Notice how that feels."

3. Undesirable factors, such as tense throat, too much expansion
of the chest, the slowly moving fix between the diaphragm and
the abdominal muscles, etc., should be eliminated. As these factors
are isolated, the teacher should continually emphasize the new feel
by telling the student, "That sounds better—notice how it feels."
Gradually, through a composite of mental understanding, continued physical practice or repetition, and judgment based upon manifested aural results, the student can distill his previously inhibited
breathing to the most simple action.

It is beneficial for the teacher to have many dramatic and color-
ful analogies at his command when describing the feel of correct
breathing. Many times just the right word picture at the right time
will unlock a mental or muscular door for the student.

The writer wishes to emphasize that *thinking* about correct
breathing and *understanding the process* of correct breathing are
a necessary and excellent beginning, but cannot of themselves produce the desired results. It is necessary to educate the nervous
system by performance, or *doing*. The body will learn irrespective
of the functions of the higher brain. The seat of muscular motor
memory is not in the cerebrum. An act can be inhibited by the
higher reasoning processes, but real learning comes in the per-

forming of the act. With practice, the voluntary, conscious feel of the act can become involuntary. For example, after the necessary movements for driving an automobile are learned, it is possible for one to carry on an animated conversation on profound subjects while driving and pay little or no attention to the many muscular coordinations necessary to perform the act of driving. An example of learning without the aid of deep reasoning processes is that of the child who is just beginning to walk. He does not read a book and find out all the kinesthetic principles of walking before he can do it! He gets to his feet and tries again and again until he gets the natural feel of the movement. Later, his reasoning process can lead his walking to certain speeds, lengths of pace, etc. Most performing artists, either in theater, art, dance, or athletics, have usually isolated and then relegated to involuntary action certain of the basic movements of their art. When performing they think as little as possible about these actions so as to foster uninhibited movement. In playing the oboe, the correct muscular actions are usually relegated to an involuntary state so that the mind can be free to foster artistic musical concepts.

2

Articulation

THIS CHAPTER WILL discuss fundamental methods of articulation (the method or manner of the joining of notes) and offer some pedagogical aids to learning these fundamentals. The manner of tonguing affects reed styles because the player must have a reed that will allow him to articulate well. Depending upon the use of his tongue and his breathing habits, the player may alter his reed style by altering the resistance, size, and shape of opening, or the length of the tip of the reed.

Many oboists are of the opinion that the use of the tongue at the instant the reed starts to vibrate is one of the most critical moments in tone production, because as the tone begins, so will it continue, unless some change is made. The fundamental principle of starting and stopping notes on the oboe is based upon (1) constant breath support and (2) the action of the tongue, as in pronouncing the word "toot." The player takes a breath; then, during the instant between the inhalation and the start of the exhalation, he puts his tongue on the reed. The upper tip of the tongue goes to the tip of the reed, keeping the cane from vibrating. In the instant after the tongue has been placed on the reed, the abdominal muscles compress the air behind the tongue *with enough force to balance the resistance of the reed* (little resistance and small opening may be desirable) *and just a bit more to stabilize the pitch, timbre, and volume level.* This process is carried out in conjunction with the forming of the embouchure. The tongue is withdrawn, the tone sounds for the required length of time, the tongue is replaced, and the tone stops. The pressure of the air remains pushing against the tongue while it is on the reed if only one note follows the first or if there is a chain of notes.

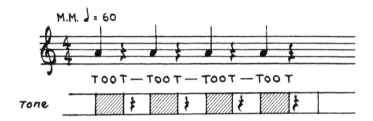

FIG. 5 Fundamental articulation

In figure 5, note that the outside "edges" of the tone remain the same size. The tones begin at this constant size and neither make a crescendo into a tone nor explode into a tone as in figure 8. The notes end at the same size at which they began. The two effects just mentioned (crescendo and sforzando) have their place in music along with other articulation effects but should be regarded as variations of the fundamental. The fundamental only requires that the tone simply start and stop. Most students find that consistency in this exercise, over the entire range of the instrument and at different speeds, legato and staccato, is more difficult than they first expect. But it is a necessary technique and has the ultimate artistic performance of music to recommend it. Artist-players can maintain the same timbre and size of tone whether they play legato or staccato, because they conceive of a continuous tone, articulated only by the tongue.

In figure 5 it should also be noted that the end of one tone is the *preparation* for the beginning of the next tone. The length of the tone is determined by the length of time that the tongue is *off* the reed. The length of the rest is determined by the length of time that the tongue is *on* the reed.

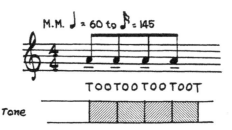

FIG. 6 Fundamental legato

Figure 6 is an illustration of legato articulation. The end of the tone is the beginning of the next tone. There is no space between tones. This fundamental articulation can be effected at different speeds and with different syllables, e.g., "duud" or "guug." However, as a fundamental, "toot'" is the recommended syllable.

Figure 7 illustrates staccato. A very important point regarding simple staccato is that each note should be *stopped* with the tongue. So many immature players only *start* notes. The ends of their notes just trail off into a sort of gray area that is devoid of conscious control. If the player wishes to use as a calculated effect the conception that tones only *start*, it is certainly permissible; but the writer considers this an effect and, consequently, a variation of the fundamental.

The only other way to release or stop a note, other than with the tongue ("toot" or "tunt"), is to reduce the breath support and allow the reed to stop vibrating. When this is done, the embouchure, by contracting a little, must usually compensate for the changes of pitch (that sinking pitch effect at the end of the note)

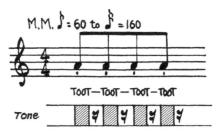

FIG. 7 Fundamental staccato

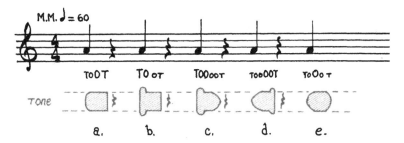

FIG. 8 Variations of the fundamental

and timbre that accompany the reduction of support. Lessening the air pressure is a legitimate and preferable way to stop notes under circumstances such as (1) the ending of a note after a long diminuendo or (2) the ends of certain *pp* phrases. A good way to practice this release is to use the syllable "who" or "too" to play quarter notes at a metronome marking of 60 beats per minute, as illustrated in figure 5, but with a diminuendo on the end of the notes.

Some players wish to achieve a nice, *round* sort of staccato (fig. 8), which has life and resonance. This is achieved not by being vague about the ending of the staccato note but by using the syllable "tunt" when tonguing and by withdrawing the tongue and replacing it on the right or left *corner* of the reed instead of stopping it "dead center." Sometimes it is advantageous to allow the air to continue through the reed during the space between staccato notes.

Some other variations of fundamental tonguing are illustrated in figure 8. There are many others that can be created by using the permutations of crescendo and diminuendo and small (*p*), medium (*mf*), and large (*sfz*) beginnings and endings of tones imposed upon the basic body and length, as in figure 5.

Some variations in articulation are illustrated in figures 9 and 10. The principle remains the same in all the additional common articulation patterns that are not illustrated here, such as: slur three and tongue one, tongue one and slur three, slur two sets of two, etc.; thus, it is not considered important to give specific illustrations of all the possible combinations.

The writer has consciously avoided using the word "attack" in this discussion of articulation, preferring instead "beginning of the tone." "Attack" is actually a misnomer, implying that the tongue attacks the reed by approaching, touching, and then withdrawing from it to start the tone. The word might also carry some conno-

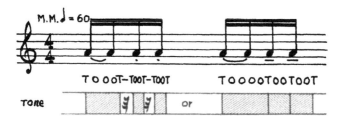

Fig. 9 Variations of articulation

Fig. 10 Variations of articulation

tation of violence, which is probably not advantageous to playing the oboe. The syllable that results from "attacking" a tone is "oot-too" rather than "toot." It is, of course, impossible to start a tone effectively with this combination of "ooo" and "too." It is very possible to start with "ooo," but the following "too," then, is an unwanted articulation and we get a double beginning, so to speak. Fundamentally, the tone should begin when the tongue is *withdrawn* ahead of the air pressure, which has already been built up enough to ensure the proper air velocity to excite the reed at a desired level.

ARTICULATION RELATED TO TIMBRE

The actual instant of the beginning of the tone is of some importance. To repeat, as the tone begins (in timbre), so will it continue, unless the performer is able to change it, which sometimes can be an unwanted, superfluous, noticeable aural effect. Proper balance of air pressure and the correct use of the tongue are mandatory *before* the tone starts.

Timbre varies with air pressure (velocity). If the air pressure remains as stable as possible during long or short notes, legato or staccato spacing between notes, or slurred notes, the timbre will remain less changeable. Therefore, a solid, steady, basic tonal quality that is capable of meeting the requirements of the musical situation is dependent in part upon constant breath support and the use of the tongue as outlined above. They work hand in hand.

The necessity for ease of articulation can affect the reed by causing the player to modify the reed opening and the amount of cane proportionately removed from the back, tip, and lay of the reed (figure 11 defines these four areas). This modification can result in a reed of different dimensions or style.

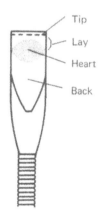

FIG. 11 The four areas of the reed

3

The Embouchure

THE EMBOUCHURE AFFECTS the way a player cuts his reed, because the lips actually cover, to varying degrees, the vibrating surface of the cane. The degree of coverage affects the timbre of the sound by allowing more or fewer of the high overtones to sound in the composite tone. If a reed, either by the player's desire or natural physical propensity, is normally covered quite extensively by the lips, the tone or timbre of a given reed will tend to be darker (less brilliant) sounding. Thus, an inherently brighter reed might be more desirable in order to compensate for the amount of lip coverage. Conversely, if a reed is normally *not* covered very much by the embouchure, it might be necessary to adjust the cut of the reed toward an inherently darker timbre in order to compensate for the lack of coverage. Each player will have his "normal" amount of coverage, depending upon the physical makeup of his embouchure. Some players will have thicker lips and, consequently, will have inherently more coverage. Some will have thinner lips and less coverage. Some players consciously try to play with more or less than normal coverage, depending upon the amount of control of timbre and/or volume that they wish.

The word "embouchure" has been borrowed from the French language and means "opening." Oboists and other wind players use the term rather loosely to mean the lips, the Orbicularis oris muscle (that muscle which surrounds the lips), and the supporting muscles of the face. It should be noted that the red part of the lips is not part of a muscle; it is a fleshy fold of mucous membrane and skin. The Orbicularis oris muscle is surrounded or covered by this membrane and actually controls the red part of the lips. The membrane is thick enough to form a pad all around the reed when the mouth assumes a whistling position and the lips turn inward *equally* over the teeth. The corners of the mouth should be drawn slightly inward to facilitate this padding or bunching of the lips. But they should not be drawn in so far as to force the lips back out of the mouth. The upper and lower teeth must be parted enough to accommodate the bunched lips. The teeth and jaws form the foundation for the lips but do not usually exert actual pressure on the reed. The muscles control the reed and can do it best if not inhibited by biting. As the mouth is opened to accommodate the lips, the lower jaw should swing comfortably downward and backward.

In this writer's opinion, the "smile" type of embouchure results in less pad for the reed, a brighter sound, less control, and more biting.

The place, or point, on the lips where the reed is initially set is used as a guide for how far the reed will eventually go into the mouth. Generally, if we place the reed about halfway inward on the red part of the lower lip, it will be at about the right place after the lips are rolled over the teeth. This initial setting of the reed is normally at about the point where both the upper and lower lips meet if the mouth is closed in normal position. The reed and both lips can touch at the same point and roll inward together without letting the reed slip on the lips. It should be emphasized that the upper lip and lower lip should balance each other in area when turned over the teeth, because a pronounced overbite on the reed tends to make the upper-register notes get progressively flatter in pitch.

Many times a student is given misleading advice by being told, "Place the reed about halfway on the red part of the lower lip and roll it inward." Very often what actually happens is that the lower lip gets rolled in farther than the upper, resulting in an overbite. The writer prefers to start the reed from between both lips and turn both lips *equally* over the teeth, as was outlined in the para-

FIG. 12 Correct pressure points on the reed (profile)   FIG. 13 Incorrect pressure points on the reed   FIG. 14 Reed angle in relation to teeth

graph above. Sometimes a player must make a conscious effort to pull his upper lip over his teeth, especially if he has a short upper lip or long upper teeth.

Figure 12 shows the correct pressure points on the reed. Note that the lips cover the most vulnerable, delicate, vigorously vibrating parts of the reed, namely, part of the tip, all of the lay, and only a part of the back. The embouchure can supply the greatest amount of control when it is in this position. Playing with too much reed in the mouth, with the lips on the hard back of the reed, causes less control simply because the tip and lay are uncovered and vibrating freely in the mouth with no lip to cover and temper them.

Figure 13 illustrates incorrect pressure points on the reed, which are usually caused by too much overbite, too much lower lip rolled inward in relation to the upper lip, or not enough upper lip pulled down over the teeth. This position usually causes oboists to play increasingly flatter as the notes go higher in the upper register. It also binds the necessary slight inward and outward movement of the embouchure. Another undesirable factor of this type of embouchure is that usually the top side of the lay and tip of the reed are laid bare. Therefore, the player does not have the control that he needs over this portion of the cane. Oboists have little enough control over all the aspects of oboe playing at best. Every advantage, however slight, is welcome.

Figure 14 illustrates the angle at which the oboe should be held in relation to the teeth. It should be held at approximately a 90° angle from an imaginary vertical line drawn through the upper and lower front teeth. If a player has a pronounced overbite, either inherent or acquired, he will hold the oboe down a little farther, that is, closer to his body, and, conversely, a player with only a little overbite will normally hold the oboe farther from the body. If the oboe is held too close to the body in relation to the teeth, it pushes the top blade of the reed into the upper lip and chokes or stifles vibration of the reed. If the oboe is held too straight out in relation to the teeth, the reed vibration can be stifled against the lower lip. The tip of the tongue should be able to touch the tip of the reed, and, by moving upward and downward slightly, it should also be able to touch the upper and lower lips that have been turned inward.

The comparatively "round" embouchure, with equal pressure points on the reed and the lips turned equally over the teeth with no biting, allows for a freedom of movement or a certain amount of "fluidity" of the center of the embouchure. This movement allows a little more reed to be taken into the mouth for playing in the upper register (helping to close the reed aperture) and allows a little less reed in the mouth, which usually facilitates playing in the lower register (allowing the reed aperture to open). The center of the embouchure actually moves slightly inward or outward, but the reed should not move on the lips.

THE FUNCTIONS OF THE EMBOUCHURE

Many and varied uses have been ascribed to the embouchure. Some players regard embouchures and their uses as bordering on the mystic and supernatural, while others hold that their importance is highly overrated, that it does not matter particularly how the embouchure functions; if the reed is good, the sound will be good. Some players are physically better equipped in this department than others. Some, through the accident of nature, may not be so well endowed but learn through practice to use what embouchure they have to even greater advantage. Actually, there are relatively few things that an embouchure can do: (1) the embouchure focuses air into the reed and keeps it from leaking around the reed; (2) it can tighten and close the opening of the reed, or it can, by relaxing muscular tension, allow the opening of the reed to return to its original size; (3) it can cover more or less of the tip and lay of the reed; (4) it can take more reed into the mouth, which closes the opening, or it can let some reed out of the mouth, which allows the opening to get larger; (5) it can make use of combinations of (2), (3), and (4), in varying degrees. The importance of these functions should not be minimized, but functions should not be ascribed to the embouchure that it cannot fulfill.

The pitch is raised when the opening of the reed is closed, either by the embouchure drawing around it or when more reed is taken into the mouth. This not only changes the pitch but can also change the timbre by producing a more brilliant sound. Sharpness is usually associated with brilliance, and flatness with less brilliance. The reverse is also true—the pitch gets lower when the opening of the reed is allowed to open, either by relaxing the embouchure or by allowing less reed in the mouth.

The reed is wedge-shaped: the opening of the cane at the tip of the reed is smaller than the opening of the cane where it joins the elliptical end of the staple. Figure 15 illustrates the point that, if more reed is taken into the mouth and the embouchure or "O" remains the same, the flexible wedge of cane can, because of its elasticity, cause the aperture of the reed to spring open, relax, or return to its inherent physical shape. The size of the aperture at the tip of the reed (the degree to which it conforms to its inherent physical shape) can be governed by the width of the shape, the hardness of the cane, the cut of the reed, or the dimension of the staple.

The embouchure will not "play" the reed or "make" the tone. Air under pressure is the only agent that can cause the reed to vibrate. The embouchure should remain completely passive except

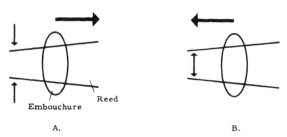

FIG. 15 The principle of the wedge

when performing the functions described at the beginning of this section. The term *controlled relaxation* can be aptly used to describe the state of the embouchure.

"We never get a good reed; we just learn to play on the bad ones." This statement, ascribed to Tabuteau, has much truth in it, thanks to the adaptability of the embouchure. We know that some players, if given a few moments with a "bad" reed, can make it sound better. Because of their ability, either learned or natural, to sense the good and bad qualities of a reed and adjust their embouchure and other tone production habits, they are able to get the best from the reed. This adjustment of the embouchure is very important when one considers that whenever an oboist changes reeds he changes the entire mouthpiece. Contrast this situation to that of the flutist or brass player, who has his problems also, but who can at least play on the same mouthpiece and know that he will get basically the same response and tone quality from day to day. Or contrast the oboist with the string player who does not have the mouthpiece problem at all, even though he also has problems peculiar to his own instrument.

As regards the adaptability of the embouchure, it should be noted that the amount of adjustment that the embouchure can make is limited. The embouchure cannot change the basic resistance and acoustical properties built into the reed; it can (as we shall see) only control the timbre to some degree. This movement, flexibility, or adaptability of the embouchure is necessary and certainly useful at times, but in order to be most effective for artistic playing, it should be coupled with an individualized reed. The reed should complement the embouchure so that the latter can operate in the most efficient physical manner. One should not have to "fight" the reed. By making his own reeds, the oboist can suit his peculiarities of tone production and instrument, become consistent in his use of embouchure and reed style, and raise his performance ability.

Two other points should be noted in conjunction with the embouchure. When playing, the chin should neither be "bunched" nor "pointed"—just normal. If the jaw is down and back as it should be, the chin will recede a little. The second point is that the air should be thought of as being focused behind the front upper teeth. This image helps to concentrate the sound.

THE EFFECT OF EMBOUCHURE ON TIMBRE

Probably the greatest effect the embouchure can have on timbre, and consequently the scrape of the reed, is its being able to uncover the reed, which causes marked change in the overtone structure (timbre). The amount of change is dependent upon the variation of the amount of coverage. The changing of the opening of the reed by the embouchure causes timbre change also. When these possibilities for timbre change are coupled with variation of air pressure, the timbre variations are compounded. Change of timbre is particularly apparent when one plays and watches an oscilloscope tube. Minute changes of embouchure and breath pressure, even for diminuendo and crescendo, are readily noticeable in the change of the wave pattern. After observing these fluctuations for a short time, the player usually begins to detect aurally subtle differences in his tonal quality that heretofore were not noticed. To describe timbre variation in words (which can be misleading), it can be said that as the player puts progressively more reed in the mouth, allowing the reed to slip on the lip, uncovering the tip and lay more and more, the timbre tends to get brighter, more brilliant, more reedy, harder, glassy, more wild, and sounds less controlled. All these words and many others could describe the timbre, depending upon the ideas, background, and vocabulary of the listener. It is also possible that the timbre change just described could be a desirable temporary change for effect or for playing on certain reeds. But playing with the reed far in the mouth might not be desirable as a matter of continuing policy. When less reed is in the mouth, there is more coverage of the wildly vibrating tip area, and thus the timbre sounds darker, less brilliant, less wild, less reedy, and more controlled and pleasant.

In the logical order of tone production that we have been following, this is the place where one would normally expect a chapter on reeds and their relation to timbre, instrument, technique of playing, and styles of reedmaking. But other factors in the chain of tone production, as yet undiscussed, affect reeds and the styles of reedmaking, and the writer feels that these should be considered before rather than after the chapter on reeds. Reeds can then be discussed by referring the reader to material that he has already read—not to material that will come later. Therefore, reeds and reed styles will be discussed in chapters 7 and 8.

4

The Instrument

THE NEXT IMPORTANT link to be investigated in the chain of sound production that influences the timbre and technique, and therefore the reed styles of the oboe player, is the instrument and its acoustical properties. All the factors of playing (breathing, embouchure, reed, etc.) are closely interrelated, and the instrument itself is no exception. It is a tremendously important link in the chain, being as it is the actual resonating body or vehicle for the amplification of the vibrations of the reed. It greatly affects the ultimate tonal quality. In the following discussion, it will be seen that the reed, in its evolution, gets proportionately narrower as the bore of the instrument gets smaller. As a result of this development, the sound changes from the loud shawm tone to the comparatively pleasant tone of the baroque true oboe and thence to the silvery penetrating sound of the modern instrument.

HISTORICAL BACKGROUND

This writer feels that he cannot add to the excellent work done by Baines, Bate, Halfpenny, and Marx (see Bibliography) on the details of the history of the instrument, and he therefore refers the reader to the outstanding works of these fine writers for an indepth history. The following is only a short and perhaps oversimplified sketch of a complicated development, with emphasis only on the basic evolution of the instrument and the reed. But it will serve as a bit of necessary background to the present-day reed situation, because the reed and the oboe have been directly affected by each other over the centuries. This mutual influence is one of the important bases of our ideas; indeed, it constitutes much of our potential for the achievement of a particular timbre and an adequate technique.

SURNA

The beginning double-reed principle is lost in antiquity. Though ancient history is not deemed entirely relevant to this book, we should note that most authorities agree that the oboe-type instrument (double reed with conical bore) reached Europe in the form of the Middle Eastern shawm, *surna* (zurnah, samr), about the time of the Crusades.[1] The *surna* was made of wood with six or seven finger holes, was conical of bore, had a trumpetlike bell, and varied in length and pitch in different countries. The sound could vary, depending upon how hard the instrument was blown and what material was used for the reed. The *surna* reed could be made of rush, corn stalk or leaf, straw, pala grass, palm leaf, or other suitable material. The reed was so pliable that, if the lips came into contact with it, the reed would stop vibrating, hence the uncontrolled reed sound. The *surna* had a loose metal disc with a hole in the middle, sometimes a coin, against which the player put his lips, with the reed extending completely into the mouth; the reed was "incapsuled" and uncontrolled by the lips.[2]

SHAWM

During the twelfth and thirteenth centuries a change took place in the dimensions of the oboe-type instrument, especially in the blowing apparatus. As the shawm[3] developed in Europe from the *surna*, the one-piece body of the instrument became longer, and the reed, a bit longer and slightly more narrow. The *surna* fell more and more into disuse as the shawm gained in popularity.

The shawm also made use of the pirouette (disc), but it was fashioned in such a way that the instrument should be considered a quasi-capsule instrument instead of a capsule instrument like the *surna* and the krumhorn. The pirouette was much closer to the reed than was the disc of the *surna*. Its placement, coupled with the use of more rigid reed cane (to be discussed momentarily), made it possible to touch the base of the reed with the lips, thereby allowing partial control of the reed and also making the upper octave easier to play. But with the *surna*, pitch, dynamics, and timbre were actually uncontrollable, except by varying the air pressure.

Now, as to the actual mean decibel level generated by the two instruments, the shawm reed, we are told, was usually made of *Arundo donax L.*, the same species of the grass family that is still used today for single- and double-reed instruments. *Arundo donax* of southern Europe is considerably more rigid than rush, palm leaf, or maize. It would seem, therefore, that the shawm was basically a louder instrument than the *surna* because of the material used for reeds, if for no other reason.

The middle of the thirteenth century to the middle of the seventeenth century is the era of the shawm. However, there is some overlapping of time between the *surna*-type instruments, the shawm, and the "French hautbois." As with other historical developments, it is impossible to delineate exactly when one type of instrument is no longer used and a new instrument takes over. To paraphrase and repeat an often used metaphor, the seeds of a new era are sprouting and growing while the blossoms of the preceding one are fading. The shawm stayed in use, declining gradually until well into the eighteenth century, while the new French hautbois was born (ca. 1657) and developed during the second half of the seventeenth century. In fact, there are areas of Europe and Asia where the shawm and *surna* are still in use today.[4]

Suffice it to say here that the question of whether the words *haut* (high) and *bas* (low) pertained to pitch or to volume appears to have been settled to the satisfaction of at least several leading musicologists. The shawm family was a member of that group of instruments that were called *haut*, meaning *loud*. Other names for the shawm include shalme, schalmey, hautbois, hoboy, wait, and piffaro. Some of these names, especially hautbois and hoboy, have led some to believe that they were the true "French hautbois," whereas they were actually shawms. The new oboe was also called *hautbois* in France, *hoboy* in England, and *oboe* in Italy.

OBOE

According to most authorities, the true French hautbois,[5] i.e., the successor to the shawm and the instrument from which our present-day oboe stems, was originated a year or so before 1660 at the court of Louis XIV. There is no documentary evidence of this contention, but the circumstantial evidence seems to lead to the logical conjecture that Jean Hotteterre I, perhaps with the help of Michel Philidor, actually invented the French hautbois.[6] The new oboe was probably used in Lully's *Ballet de l'amour malade* of 1657 in its *Concert champêtre de l'epoux* and *overture;* also, it possibly appeared in the same composer's *Un Charivari grotesque* of *le Mariage forcé* of 1664. The first mention of an oboe in a Lully score appears in 1664 in *Les Plaisirs de l'Isle Enchantée*, containing a *Marche de le dieu Pan et sa suite*. Oboes were played in Lully's music for Molière's *Le Bourgeois Gentilhomme* in 1670. Most texts mention Cambert's opera *Pomone* of 1671 as the first instance of orchestration that actually specified the use of the true oboe.[7]

In the opinion of Joseph Marx,[8] the new instrument came about as the result of changes in reed style, music, and performing organizations, and because of the need for a controlled, softer, indoor, concert-type instrument.[9]

The new French oboe had three sections instead of retaining the one-piece construction of the older shawm.[10] The bore was slightly narrower than that of the shawm and had less flair to the cone; double holes for the little fingers evolved; the diameter of the tone holes was reduced; and the outward appearance was changed by the addition of the elegant turnery. But perhaps the most important change was the discarding of the pirouette for the new-style reed, the tip of which was actually covered and controlled by the lips.

For the first time, the music world had a treble double-reed instrument with a controllable sound. The tone was more refined than the old "outdoor," "haut," rather undignified band shawm. And, above all, oboists were able to perform in the same musical fashion as the other refined instruments of the time, whether in consort, in an orchestra, or indoors. The tone of the new oboe was closely akin to our present-day tone, but with fewer high harmonics because of the wider reed—not wild, loud, or reedy. (The earliest known width for a true oboe reed is 9.5 millimeters; an overall reed length of 98 millimeters was mentioned by Talbot ca. 1696.[11] These figures compare to our present-day 6.88 millimeter average width and 69.51 millimeter average length.) The notion that the baroque oboe tone was wild and loud is an unfortunate misconception, perpetrated by unknowing or careless writers who failed to draw an accurate line between the shawm and the French hautbois.

The new instrument enjoyed rather immediate success and soon spread to other countries. It was probably introduced to England by the oboist James Paisible, when Cambert directed the court masque of *Calisto* in 1674,[12] three years after the appearance of the instrument in the orchestration of *Pomone*.

During the eighteenth century the then new oboe developed into the two- and three-keyed "baroque" style instrument[13] (late seventeenth century) and subsequently into the "classical" instrument (late eighteenth century). Probably the most important changes were the progressive narrowing of the bore until about the time of Mozart and the addition of six to ten more keys shortly thereafter.[14] Baines states that eighteenth-century reeds for these instruments seem to have been broader than those of today, measuring from 8 to 10 millimeters.[15] Garnier,[16] ca. 1800, prescribes a reed tip 8 millimeters wide and an overall reed length of 70 millimeters. Regarding this, Warner states, "It would seem reasonable . . . that around 1780 the old broad reed evolved into the narrow type."

The nineteenth century brought great changes from the baroque and classical two- and three-keyed oboes of the preceding era. Before the turn of the century, C. A. Grenser and J. F. Grundmann of Dresden experimented with added keys. Later came the innovations of Henri Brod, Theobald Boehm, A. M. R. Barret, and the new systems of the Triébert family. Frédéric Triébert (1813–78) was probably the most innovative oboe maker of his family, which included his father, Guillaume Triébert (1770–

1848), and his brother, Charles Triébert (1810–67). At the time
of his death, Frédéric had perfected his Systéme 6. The famous
François Lorée, before he established his own oboe-making business, was a workman for the Triébert firm and modified the Systéme 6 to the Systéme A6. In 1882 the Systéme A6 was adopted
by Georges Gillet as the "Conservatoire" (of Music, Paris) model
oboe. In 1906 A. L. Lorée, son of François, further perfected the
"covered-hole" key plates that Gillet and F. Lorée had devised
earlier.[17] The "Conservatoire" system has since been improved by
such makers as Rigoutat, Laubin, Louis, and Howarth. The main
advances of the nineteenth century consist of a further narrowing
and slightly different shape of the bore, a change of material from
boxwood and rosewood to ebony or grenadilla wood, a further sta-
bilization of pitch, the addition of keys, better placement of tone
holes, and further narrowing of the reed.

The German-type oboe (Heckel), with the larger bore, became
divided from the French type around 1800 and still is very much
in evidence in Vienna (Zuleger)[18] and Russia.[19] It is characterized
by a timbre that blends very well with other instruments.

In summary, over the centuries (almost eight hundred years) the
mechanical and tonal character of the soprano double-reed instrument of the Western world (the oboe type) has changed considerably, progressing from *surna* to shawm and thence to the
oboe and its various stages of evolution. This has been due only
in part to mechanical and acoustical advances, because changes in
musical styles have also made demands upon the instrument, and
technical advances of the instrument have in turn allowed for its
greater usefulness to the composer. Also, the musical tastes prevalent in certain countries during a particular era have influenced
the types of oboes and artistic concepts of oboe timbres prevalent
in other countries. A particularly good example of this phenomenon is in the case of France during the mid-seventeenth and mid-
nineteenth centuries.

The future will no doubt bring more change. It is possible that
our present-day music will sound as different in the concert halls
of the future as sixteenth- and seventeenth-century music sounds
in the concert halls of today. Traditionalists then will hold with
the past and present, as they do now, and there will also be those
who prefer something different or new.

Basically, over the years the oboe bore has become narrower, the reed has become controllable by the lips after being freed from the pirouette, and reeds have become narrower as the bore has gotten smaller. More keys have been added to facilitate technique and intonation. Heavier wood is used for the resonating body. Thanks to, in part, the principles of Boehm, Helmholtz, and the advancing science of acoustics, tone holes have undergone much development in spacing, size, and undercutting, which has helped intonation and response. All these changes have affected the timbre of the instrument and, therefore, the cut of the reed.

THE ACOUSTICS OF THE OBOE

The previous historical discussion will serve as background material to understanding present-day oboe reed styles. It will also be helpful to discuss the acoustics of the oboe in order to understand more about the factors that can affect contemporary reed styles. A brief discussion of acoustics will also bring out certain other factors that may be attributed to the instrument in the production of its characteristic and individualized timbre. The field of musical acoustics is a very complex one, and the reader interested in more detail, formulae, etc., should consult the standard texts on the subject. Those acoustical aspects included here are presented in untechnical fashion and are limited to those which, in varying degrees, have direct influence on the final tonal results.

The oboe is a sound system comprising three joined units: (1) the air-producing and resonating cavities of the player's body; (2) the reed or excitor; and (3) the body of the instrument or resonator. With any instrument employing a mechanical reed, practically a complete interruption of air flow takes place each time the reed closes; thus, the oral cavity of the player enters intimately into the acoustic action of the instrument. The role of (1), the player's body, in tone production has been discussed in the preceding chapters. The role of (2), the reed, and (3), the resonator, will be discussed next.

The action of the double reed in interrupting the air stream is depicted in figure 16.[20]

The basic physical principle illustrated in figure 16 will not vary with the style of the reed. But the *mode of vibration* of the total

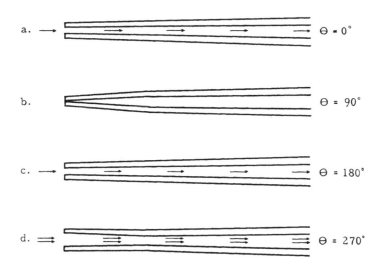

FIG. 16 The principle of the mechanical
double reed

reed and of its parts—that is, the wave patterns that result in the relative number and distribution of partials[21]—will vary according to the way the reed is cut.

The symbol in figure 16 marks one of a set of sequential points in the most basic vibration pattern of a double reed. The point of initial equilibrium is θ equals 0 degrees, and the sequence is complete at 360 degrees (θ equals 0 degrees). The θ points also correspond to points on a graph of a simple harmonic motion, for example, a single transverse wave in a string, or a single longitudinal wave in an air column. The sequence is repeated at the resonant frequency of the system, for example, at A 440 cycles per second the sequence repeats 440 times per second.

With the reeds in the normal position (fig. 16a, θ equals 0 degrees), air is forced through the opening between the reeds. The high velocity of the air through the opening reduces the pressure between the reeds, in accordance with Bernoulli's theorem.[22] Because of reduced air pressure, the reeds are forced closer together (the air molecules pressing on the outside of the reed are able to collapse the blades against their own elasticity into the area of less pressure), so that the aperture through which the air moves is reduced, thereby reducing the air flow. This effect is illustrated in figure 16b, θ equals 90 degrees. When the air flow is reduced by the constricted passage, the internal pressure on the two reeds then increases, and the reeds spring back to the original position, as shown in figure 16c, θ equals 180 degrees.

Owing to the inertial energy of the reeds, they move beyond the original position to the position shown in figure 16d, θ equals 270 degrees. Now the opening is very large and the air flow is correspondingly large. Under these conditions, the internal pressures on the reeds are again small, and, as a result, the reeds return to the normal position of Figure 16a, θ equals 0 degrees, and the cycle of events is repeated at the resonant frequency of the system.

The variation of flow in the air stream occurs at the frequency of the vibration of the reed. The throttling action of the reeds converts a steady air stream into a pulsating one of the saw-tooth type, which, when plotted as a sine wave, contains the fundamental and all the harmonics. These variations of air flow form "standing waves," which are altered and reinforced by the resonances in the tube of the oboe. Sound waves in a column of air (enclosed by a tube) are *longitudinal*, as distinguished from the visual *transverse* or *latitudinal* waves of a stretched string. They are waves or relative compression and rarefaction and are therefore produced by displacements of the air particles back and forth in the same line of travel that the waves themselves follow. If the frequency of these waves is constant and properly adjusted with relation to the length of the air column, their reflections from the ends of the column of air will be superposed on the unreflected waves, producing *standing waves*, which greatly enforce the original vibration. "Partials" are produced by standing waves vibrating in mathematical segments of the fundamental.

The overall tube of the oboe is conical with certain slight deviations along the body of the cone and with a slight flare at the mouth. The acoustical length of the air column is controlled by finger holes and keys that operate valves on the holes. These openings alter the resonant frequencies of the air column corresponding to the musical scale.

The instrument tube serves principally as a resonator that

strongly reinforces certain components of the comparatively random sound produced by the reed, thus causing the instrument to sound a single predominant frequency. An *open* pipe, whether it be conical or cylindrical, can produce a tone containing even- and odd-numbered partials. Truly *stopped* pipes will produce, at least theoretically, a tone containing only odd-numbered partials, as does the clarinet,[23] which overblows the twelfth (not the octave).

According to Philip Bate, the oboe is generally considered to be an open pipe, even though it has stopped-pipe, standing-wave characteristics. There are both demonstrations and mathematical proofs that a *conical* tube closed at its vertex (stopped closed pipe) resonates to the entire series of harmonic overtones, i.e., to the musical octave, twelfth, fifteenth, etc. These are also characteristics of a cylindrical pipe open at both ends—an open pipe. Therefore, the oboe (conical tube) *acts as an open pipe* (resonating all partials and overblowing the octave), *but* it has the standing-wave characteristics of a *stopped* pipe, in that it has a node at the stopped end of the tube and a standing-wave loop at or near the open end of the tube.

Now, the *scale* of a tube is the ratio of its diameter compared to its length. Harmonic development (the number of partials) is usually greater in small tubes. Therefore, the small scale of the oboe tube, i.e., the ratio of diameter to length of the tube, combined with the conical bore, allows it to produce a tone rich in partials. This quality is especially noticeable in the lower registers. The tone tends to have less harmonic development as the notes go higher, because the scale of the pipe enlarges in relation to the effective length of the pipe. The pitch is regulated, as was mentioned above, by the closing or opening of the laterally bored tone holes, which either adds or subtracts from the effective length of the tube, causing the pitch to go up or down—the shorter the tube the higher the pitch; the longer the tube, the lower the pitch.

TIMBRE

Timbre is that characteristic of a tone which depends upon the richness of its harmonic structure. The timbre of a tone is expressed in the number, intensity, distribution, and phase relations of the partials that make up the tone or "klang." Timbre, then, may be said to be the instantaneous cross section of the tone quality.

There are six physical characteristics that determine timbre: (1) the number of partials present in a tone; (2) the distribution of the partials; (3) the relative intensity of the partials; (4) the inharmonic partials; (5) the formant; and (6) the total intensity. These characteristics can be modified (changing the timbre) by any of the three units that join to make the acoustical system, the player, the reed, or the oboe. For example, an almost infinite number of possibilities can occur in the relative intensity, number, and distribution of the partials of a tone. However, when we specify an *oboe* tone, we find that most of the range of partials and their modifications lies between 500 and 1500 cycles per second and rarely goes above 7,000 cps. As to the other phenomena, the *inharmonic partials* can make the quality either richer or unpleasant. These partials are the result of out-of-tune harmonics, difference tones, summation tones, reed buzz, and air noise. In the composite oboe sound there is a *formant range* just below C″″″ (the top C on the piano) that is about four times louder than the fundamental range. This formant, it has been suggested, is what gives the oboe its characteristic sound. There is no doubt that the formant considerably affects the listener's and player's impressions of the general timbre, because of the ear's greater sensitivity to high partials coupled with greater volume. The *total intensity* of a tone also influences the timbre, because more partials are generated by the instrument at a high intensity level. In general, the higher the intensity level, the greater the number of partials that the ear can discern.

Admittedly, when the oboist is actually playing, it is doubtful that he has any real selective control over some of the above acoustical phenomena. But he can recognize the presence of them and, through this, perhaps encourage greater resonance, etc. in certain areas through modification of reeds and tone production. Over such things as partials and intensity he has quite a lot of control, as we have seen in the discussion of embouchure and respiration.

Whenever there has been a change of style of instrument or reed over the previous centuries, it has entailed a modification in one of the following factors. In other words, these factors influence the speech and timbre of the resonating body of the oboe.

1. The reed. As has been previously stated, the hollow, conical tube of the oboe will supposedly *resonate* all the partials, odd and even, but we must take into account how that sound wave is *generated. The body of the instrument cannot resonate or put into its composite sound something that is not introduced to it by the reed.* At this point the reed becomes extremely important. Within limits the reed can be cut or adjusted to *produce* a type of timbre or to change an existing timbre by varying one, all, or any combination of the six physical characteristics enumerated above. On the other hand, the resonating body can be varied to *select* timbre. These possibilities for variation, along with a mental concept of a particular sound, form the basis for particular reed styles over the world. *Reed styles have evolved in conjunction with the dimensions of the oboe in order to achieve a certain timbre and musical facility, which have been dictated by personal preference and musical demand.* These differences of preference, manifested in measurements and the like, will be brought out later, in the chapter on reed styles.

2. The shape and length of the tube. Chambering (widening) the bore near an anti-node (loop) of the note the instrument is sounding will change the pitch and timbre. The irregularity of the bore of the oboe at the wrong places can cause partials to be out of tune with the fundamental. We know that there is a certain amount of built-in (inherent) out-of-tuneness between certain partials in a composite sound. The upsetting of this balance, as through incorrect chambering, can cause destruction of the core of the sound, excessive brilliance, reediness, etc. In regard to the length of the tube, theoretically, the longer the tube, the lower the pitch will be.

3. The scale of the tube. Small-scale pipes tend to develop the higher partials. Large-scale pipes develop them less.

4. The material of which the tube is made. The density and weight of the metal or wood used in a tube influence the timbre of the tone.

5. The thickness of the material of which the pipe is made. Pipes with thin walls have greater harmonic development.

6. The diameter of the tone holes. A small hole bored higher up on the tube will produce the same pitch as a larger one placed lower. The annular effect also influences the timbre; that is, air molecules are more active near the walls of the hole than in the center.

7. The height of the sides of the tone holes. Usually, the higher the sides of the hole, the flatter the tone. Also, undercutting the underside of the tone hole will change the pitch and timbre.

8. The bell. As yet, little is known scientifically about the effect that the bell has on the oboe, but it is known from experience that bells of differing dimensions placed upon the upper two joints of the instrument can greatly change the tone and response of the total instrument. This effect probably derives from (2) above.

9. Presence or absence of the step in the bore. It is thought that this step has the effect of shortening the tube and thereby altering the intonation of the complete tube, with certain notes being affected more than others, especially those notes close to the joints where the step occurs.

10. Vent holes. Certain holes, besides sounding simple notes in the first and second registers, also serve as vents to aid the production of higher harmonics, and this calls for some compromise in the placement of the tone holes. In other words, the diameter of the hole, its position on the body of the instrument, the length, diameter, and wall thickness of the main tube, and whether or not other holes are open at the same time are all extremely interrelated.

11. Acoustical impedance. This is a property that all tubes and holes have to some degree and that can be mathematically computed. This factor, along with its components, resistance, reactance, and end correction, can help determine the placement of tone holes, the timbre, and the power of a tube.

12. Air pressure. Generally, the more air pressure used, the greater the harmonic development, because of the richer vibration pattern of the beating reeds. This relationship is true in oboe playing up to the point of diminishing returns, which is reached fairly quickly. A reed style that demands a small opening will only accept a limited amount of air before it "chokes down."

In summary, the soprano double-reed instrument has progressed from the *surna* to the shawm, the baroque-classical oboe, the nineteenth-century oboe, and finally to the modern instrument. The timbre has changed from the rather reedy oriental sound of the *surna* to the louder, undignified sound of the shawm, then to the more refined, softer, indoor, consort or orchestral sound of the French hautbois, and finally to the more sophisticated, silvery and penetrating solo tone of the modern instruments. This evolution has been accompanied with a narrowing of the reed from the short triangular reed of the *surna* to the slightly narrower and longer shawm reed (mid-thirteenth to late seventeenth centuries), thence to the even narrower and longer reed of the baroque-classical era (late seventeenth to late eighteenth centuries), which was joined to the staple. Our present nineteenth-century oboe reeds, which are, fortunately or not, far from being stabilized, are generally more narrow still than the baroque-classical reeds. Bores, in relation to length, have become smaller, with the smaller-scale pipes having a richer content of partials. Heavier woods with higher resonance peaks are being used, and oboes in general are better in tune. Because we have no actual evidence to the contrary, it is probably safe to say that mechanical advancements have made greater technical proficiency possible on our modern instruments.

Over the years styles of playing have changed as players have found it necessary to meet technical and aesthetic demands of changing musical eras, social preference, and the desires of players, composers, conductors, and public for a particular oboe tonal quality. Closely interrelated changes in the oboe, the methods of tone production of the player, and the dimensions of the reed styles have resulted from and contributed to these changes in playing styles. The primary characteristics that have been affected are set forth above, in the sections about timbre and the resonating tube.

The writer has attempted to briefly describe the factors that may be attributed to the instrument in the production of its characteristic and individualized timbre. It should be emphasized that any change of the factors presented in the sections on timbre and resonator will also affect one another. The oboe itself is an important link in the chain of tone production and, therefore, has great influence on the type of reed, or minute alterations of a type of reed, that the performer may find it necessary to use (make) in order to achieve the results he desires in the technique of playing or in the production of a certain timbre.

The instrument is a factor that is seldom exploited, although it could be of great help to a player. Most players acquire an instrument, get accustomed to it, and play it, with all its strengths and weaknesses, much too long. This situation is usually due to financial inability to experiment with instruments, lack of time, or lack of interest in acquiring a better oboe. In addition, and perhaps more important, the percentage of really excellent professional instruments produced is very small compared to the total output of oboes—at any price. Great instruments, or even very good instruments, are very difficult to find. However, many of the problems of intonation, response, and tone quality that players encounter are directly attributable to the instrument. The writer hesitates to speak only of *problems* in this regard, because some oboists seem to have relatively few problems with the embouchure, reed, or oboe. These fortunate few have usually managed to put the fundamentals—the raw materials—of playing into an exceptionally well-balanced whole. As we have seen, the oboe itself is one of these raw materials.

The next two chapters contain a discussion of several other remaining factors that enter into the chain of oboe-sound production and, therefore, affect styles of reedmaking. They have to do with the acoustical influence of the room and the psychological influence of the listener on the oboist and the timbre that he produces. These factors are not as intimately joined as the player-reed-oboe system but, nevertheless, are important to rounding out the complete cycle for the ear and mind of the player and listener.

5

The Acoustics of the Room

SOUND WAVES HAVE certain properties that can, to varying degrees, affect the timbre and the reed styles of the oboist. These properties are beats; difference tones and summation tones; simple, multiple, harmonic, and musical echo; absorption; and diffraction. Some of these properties are the result of the tone's being played in a particular room or of its being heard by a particular person under certain acoustical conditions. If the oboist played only outdoors in an open area where there were nothing to affect the sound waves emitted from the reed and resonated by the instrument, the waves would be dissipated in all directions around the player at approximately 1100 feet per second, and the art of reedmaking would be much less complicated. However, the oboist usually plays indoors, with walls, a ceiling, and a floor around him. Thus, because of angles and construction materials, sound waves take on characteristics that affect oboe timbre as it is recognized by the mind through the ear.

When one hears sound waves, they are either *direct* or *reflected.* The player and the listener hear some waves directly. These direct waves combine with reflected waves and form a composite sensation of timbre. The player hears this composite sound with the addition of some vibrations via bone conduction and some middle-ear distortion. Therefore, he hears a different timbre from the listener, who hears the composite sound *at a distance*, after it has been acted upon by absorption. reverberation, and his own physical and psychological characteristics. The relative loudness of sounds and their partials changes as the distance is changed between the sound source and the listener—one cause for differences of opinion regarding timbre among listeners at different points in a room or concert hall. Another important cause of timbre differences at given points of a room is the ratio between *direct* and *reflected* sound waves. The listener's sense of sound *presence* will be enhanced proportionately as the incidence of direct sound waves increases, provided that the material from which the reflective surfaces are made reproduces the sound honestly.

Reverberation is the continuing roll of sound (numerous overlapping multiple echoes) and can be beneficial or detrimental to timbre. Sounds can be reflected from one time up to thirty, forty, or more times, depending upon the reflective surface, the size and shape of the room, and the energy of the wave. For most rooms, a reverberation time of one to two seconds is sufficient to give a reasonable representation of tone for the oboe (again, provided that the reflective surfaces reproduce the sound honestly). Generally, too much reverberation (live room) will cause the oboist to make a darker sounding reed while too little reverberation (dead room) will cut out too many high partials and cause him to make a brighter sounding reed. The adjustment either way would effect a slight change in the way he basically cuts his reed. Reverberation can build up, lessen, or otherwise modify partials, depending upon the amount of absorption of the reflecting surface. Reverberation can cause loss of high harmonics because of atmospheric absorption. Multiple reflections can cause loss of brilliance, because the long paths travelled by the waves in their many reflections allow time for atmospheric absorption to take its toll. These effects can be modified or reversed if the higher partials of a complex sound are actually encouraged to have a much greater intensity level than the lower ones. As an example of how a sound can be built up by reverberation, in some halls the ratio of reverberant sound to direct sound may be as high as ten to one. Reinforcement by resonance of a particular room may not only strengthen or weaken an entire composite tone but may also affect certain frequency areas within the pattern of partials that make up the tone.

Absorption is the weakening of sound waves through incomplete reflection. The high partials are usually absorbed first, tending to make a sound less brilliant.

Superposition of sound waves makes it possible for a complex sound to be heard. Two or more different wave trains (series of enlarging spheres of compression and rarefaction) from one or many different instruments, voices, or other sources may exist in the air or in other media at the same time. These series of pulses will travel through each other without destroying each other. The foregoing is true except for another property of sound waves—*interference*—usually present to some degree. In effect, interference means that if two superposed wave trains are from sources having the same frequency, they can be either magnified or cancelled by each other. If these wave trains of the same frequency are in phase and meet at the same point in time and space, the sound will be louder than either single source. If a compression of one train and a rarefaction of the other train meet at the same point (out of phase), theoretically there will be silence. When one listens to a tone, there are so many wave trains setting air molecules in motion that periods of great loudness or silence are seldom heard, but one sometimes may move from or into an interference field in an acoustically inconsistent room and thereby hear some change.

Beats, difference tones, and summation tones are other properties of sound waves that can affect oboe timbre only if the oboe is sounding with another instrument. At certain intensity levels and in certain ranges of the instrument, the overtones can sound louder than the fundamental. If these harmonics are too far out of tune with themselves, it is obvious that the timbre will be changed.

Other properties of sound waves that are the result of reflection and reverberation and that can affect timbre are *simple, multiple, harmonic,* and *musical* echoes.[1] The first three probably have more effect than the last.

When sound waves are bent around obstacles, the resultant change in their direction is called *diffraction.* Long waves (lower tones and partials) persist more than short waves (higher tones and partials). Thus, imposing a person or any other appreciable object —not a small, inconsequential object—between the player and the listener will change the timbre by cutting down the high partials more than the low ones.

In theory, all the above properties of sound waves contribute to the psychological aspect of tone that we call timbre. These properties affect the composite tone to varying degrees—some of them only slightly. However, when all are added together, they form a unified quality that can govern a player's opinion of his reed. After the reed and the oboe, the most noticeable single factor that influences the player is probably the reverberation rate of the room. The acoustical properties of the room affect the balance that is given to the tone by the player, the reed, and the instrument and can cause the player to make adjustments of his reed.

6

The Listener

In CONSIDERING the listener, it is important to remember that the psychological aspects of musical perception, i.e., the senses of pitch, intensity, time, rhythm, timbre, etc., are variable factors in all people. Thus, people differ from each other not only in their psychological and aesthetic reactions to an oboe sound, but also in what they hear in the beginning. Certain distortions of hearing can alter the listener's opinion of a timbre, thereby influencing (ultimately) the player to modify a reed. The most important of these distortions are deafness, hearing sensitivity, fatigue effects, bone conduction, and middle-ear distortion.

Degrees of *deafness* can occur, and this deafness (not to be confused with *total* deafness) is usually not uniform over the entire pitch range. It may be at the low end, the upper end, or somewhere in between, and can occur in varying degrees. In other words, it is possible to have islands of silence in the total frequency range of hearing.

Hearing sensitivity varies with age; thus, we would expect a youngster to be able to hear a richer tone than, for example, a person over sixty years of age. It is doubtful that a person over forty years of age hears over 15,000 cps. An upper limit of 15,000 cps will not appreciably hinder a person's conception of oboe tone, because the upper frequency range of partials of the oboe tone seldom goes above 7,000 cps. But the lowered upper limit of frequency could affect the sensitivity of the person's ear to the higher partials and thus affect the listener's idea of the timbre. A considerable amount of confusion in pitch judgment can occur toward the upper and lower extremes of the pitch range.

The Fletcher-Munson Equal Loudness Curve shows that the ear's sensitivity varies with frequency and intensity. The upper formant and many of the partials of the oboe tone lie in the region where the ear is most sensitive. The formant of the oboe lies just below C'''', and the natural reverberation frequency of the ear canal is 2000–4000 cps. Oscilloscope analysis confirms that the high partials are quite predominant in the oboe tone, sometimes over-shadowing the fundamental, and so we say that the instrument has a very penetrating quality.

Middle-ear distortion tends to supply added partials to a pure tone. The louder the external tone, the greater the middle-ear distortion tends to be. The effect lessens as the pitch rises.

Other factors that can affect an individual's hearing are *fatigue effects* and *bone conduction*, which are self-explanatory.

SOCIOLOGICAL ACCEPTANCE OF STYLES OF PLAYING

Yet another factor enters into the delineation of reed styles, one that has to do with the listener. Oboe players in general wish to sound "good," or acceptable, in the eyes (or, in this case, in the ears) of the public or of other individuals. There are players who may say that they do not care whether or not other people like their playing, but the writer feels that the urge for social acceptance still burns within them even though they decry it. Our musical society in the United States has grown over the years to accept and prefer a certain type of oboe sound. In other words, it is thought that an oboe should sound a certain way. The opinions of others regarding style of oboe sound is conditioned in large part by what they are accustomed to hearing. In this country this tonal image has changed in the last two generations, chiefly because most of the older players of the French school have retired

from the professional orchestras of the country, and their positions
have been filled by young American oboists who use a longer
scrape reed. Oboists themselves in this country have much in common with one another, even though they disagree on many fine
points of timbre. The tendency is, of course, for this present
school of sound to perpetuate itself for a number of years into the
future, because the younger players are being taught to produce
this American type of sound with the long scrape reed, and our
musical society has grown to accept the sound. A true French,
English, or Viennese style of oboist who would come to this
country would enjoy limited success in a permanent position because he sounds different. The European simply has a different
style of playing, which he learns, prefers, and which is accepted in
his musical society. So we may say that, in order to achieve so-
cially and individually acceptable tonal results in each particular
country, the style of reed is adjusted to the method of tone production, the acoustics of the oboe, and the *accepted tonal conception.*

In the foregoing chapters the writer has discussed many of the
technical and pedagogical aspects of tone production for playing
the oboe. Insofar as possible, these aspects of tone production have
been related to timbre and technique so as to show their relationship to and influence on oboe reeds and styles of reeds. This last
chapter is the end of the chain of sound production factors, which
began with the respiration of the player and moved through the
open throat, and embouchure, the reed (discussion deferred), the
instrument, and the acoustics of the room, and ended at the ears
of the listener.

The writer feels that the material in Part I was necessary to
place the reed in the overall picture and that the reader will consequently understand more about the function and styles of reeds
as a result of having read the preceding chapters. We are now
ready to proceed to a survey of reeds of selected artist-players and
a delineation of styles based on these examples.

PART TWO

Oboe Reeds

7

Reeds of Individual Oboists

IN THIS CHAPTER the reader will find, categorized by country, biographical data from a representative group of artist-oboists and
photographs of their reeds. A delineation of styles is made in chapter 8; the reader will note when studying the photographs in this
chapter and the measurements in Table 3, chapter 9, that those
reeds of the same style (which are not necessarily limited nation-
ally) will have certain visual and dimensional characteristics in
common. These two factors, the visual and the dimensional, contribute to perhaps the most important properties of reeds—the
aural characteristics (timbre) and the playing qualities. Playing
qualities that are adequate to the musical situation are, of course, a
necessity, but one sometimes accepts some leeway in timbre. As
the reader will note, no two reeds look or measure alike. Neither
do they play exactly alike. Neither are musical or acoustical conditions, individual embouchures, or tonal concepts likely to be the
same. Consequently, two persons seldom have the same judgment
as to the excellence of a given reed. Even so, the reeds that follow
are representative examples of what present-day artists consider
"adequate" for their performing needs. It will be evident that quite
a range of styles exists, and there are even quite noticeable differences between reeds of the same style.

One should bear in mind that looking at a reed and its dimensions will give only an incomplete idea of the actual sound. Reeds respond and sound differently when played by different players and on separate instruments. It is easy to distort the sound of reeds with individual embouchures and oboes. For example, two players can play entirely different looking reeds on separate oboes and get very close to the same sound out of each of them. Also, after getting accustomed to a reed, a player, through adjustment, can usually make it sound better. Consequently, the student should not look for hard and fast rules regarding how reeds sound in relation to how they look. Each player is his own salvation in this area of reedmaking. What seems good for one person may not be good for another. In the last, artistic analysis, *one must suit his own particular needs and preferences.*

The amount of resistance to blown air pressure in the reed is a very sensitive and very important aspect of oboe playing and reedmaking. This amount of resistance built into the reed (actually, left in the reed) usually seems to be related very directly to the amount of "reediness" or "life" in the timbre. A greater resistance gives a darker sound, and a lesser resistance a brighter sound, although this is not necessarily always true. One might think that one could judge the amount of resistance in the reed by looking at the photographs or at the actual reeds, but the writer, over many years of experience with reeds, has been singularly unsuccessful in being able to judge the resistance factor in a reed (how hard it is to blow) just by looking at it or seeing its dimensions.

The writer has found that *the timbre of the reed varies in direct proportion to the amount of wood removed from the tip, lay, and back of the reed.* This relationship holds true assuming that the player conscientiously tests the reed as consistently as possible with the same oboe and embouchure.

In the plates that follow, each reed is shown first in *reflected light* and then in *silhouette.* If there is more than one example from a particular player, the reeds are grouped, and each *group* is shown first in reflected light and then in silhouette:

1   2   3   1   2   3
(in reflected light)   (in silhouette)

For the most effective view of the reed photographs, tilt the top of the book toward you. The amount of tilt will depend upon your light source.

Except for the eight most recent (1980) examples, the photographs of the reeds were made with an Auto-Graflex single-lens reflex camera with double-extension bellows. The top-lighted photographs were exposed on size 120 Panatomic X film for three seconds at F 22 using a 300-watt photoflood lamp suspended about four feet over the reed. The lamp was adjusted so that the light rays fell in such a way as to show the scrape of the reed as truly as possible; the intent was not necessarily to make them look good. The back-lighted photographs (silhouette) were exposed six seconds at F 13 on size 120 Panatomic X film. The light reflected through the reeds was supplied by a 60-watt incandescent bulb in a standard desk lamp. The bulb was approximately two inches from the reed. The prints were made with an Omega D$_2$ enlarger on Kodak Medalist paper. With the exceptions noted above, all photographs were exposed, developed, and printed under the same technical conditions. For several compelling reasons it was necessary to photograph and print the most recent examples under different technical conditions. Any photographic interpretation, conscious or unconscious, was simply an attempt to present as objective a representation as possible, through the eyes (so to speak) of one oboist. *All photographs of reeds are exactly twice life size.*

The biographical data and the pertinent remarks about the reeds were supplied by the players over a period of years. Updating the material in 1979–80 resulted in further information. It was not possible to recontact all of the contributors because of changed (unknown) addresses and deaths. However, these factors do not affect the delineation of reed styles. Information about some of the deceased players was obtained from colleagues, family, and/or friends.

The reed examples are in alphabetical order by the player's country at the time of initial contact.

The measurements of the photographed examples were made by the writer and are presented in Table 3, chapter 9. It is recommended that the reader examine Table 3 at this time.

1. AUSTRALIA

Jiri Tancibudek. Born March 5, 1921, in Prague, Czechoslovakia. At the present time (1980) Tancibudek is Reader (Associate Professor), Music Faculty, University of Adelaide, South Australia, and a member of the University of Adelaide Wind Quintet. He has held both positions since 1964. Other positions he has held include First Oboist of the Czechoslovak Philharmonic Orchestra under Raphael Kubelík from 1945 until 1950; First Oboist in Stuttgart, Germany; teacher at the Sidney State Conservatory of Music, Sidney, Australia; and First Oboist of the Victoria Symphony Orchestra (now called the Melbourne Symphony), Melbourne, Australia. He studied with Josef Děda and František Hanták, both of Prague. Tancibudek plays a Rigoutat oboe. He has at other times owned Marigaux and Howarth oboes and played a Trejbal (Czechoslovakia) oboe for many years.

Tancibudek's method of winding and scraping the cane more or less follows that of his teachers in Czechoslovakia and is considerably different from the method used in the United States. The nylon is first wound around a rather hard ball of paper about four or five inches in diameter. This ball can then be held between the knees and pulled against when wrapping the cane on the staple, thus removing the necessity for having a hook or chair upon which to tie the nylon. When one is on tour, this ball of paper can be a handy accessory. Tancibudek states that it is normal procedure to hold the cane and staple in the *right* hand while binding. This is usually done only by left-handed reedmakers in the United States, England, etc.

Probably the greatest difference between Tancibudek's method and that used in the United States is in the holding of the reed and the knife while the scraping is being done. The reed is held in the left hand, hand closed and toward the oboist's face, between thumb and forefinger, cane *toward* the body and resting on the second or index finger. The right hand holds the knife with the thumb steadying the hand by resting either on the end of the left-hand second finger or on both the second and third fingers. The knife blade is pulled toward the body, much as one would pare an apple, with the exception that the knife blade is turned upright, almost at a 90° angle to the cane, so that it scrapes rather than cuts.

The knife used for such scraping has a handle of about 4 inches and a 2 or 2½ inch, fairly heavy steel blade, which is hollow-ground only on one side. The cutting edge is curved.

The plaque resembles a miniature, triangular bassoon plaque—thin on the edges and graduated evenly up to about 1 millimeter in the center. A plaque of this shape usually fills the opening of the reed so that the blades of the reed do not have to be pressed far down onto the plaque by the thumb when one works on the lay. Excessive downward pressure of the thumb can cause one to split the blades of a reed when the conventional, thin, spring-steel plaque is used.

The two reeds represented in Plate 1 are made with Glotin staples and cane. The shape is by Delacroix and the gouge of the cane is .57–.58 mm. Tancibudek states that the scrape of these reeds is rather long because his present oboe is sharp in pitch.

Dates of information: 1958, 1980.

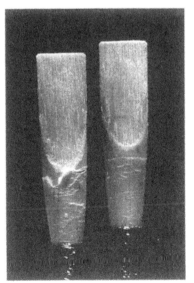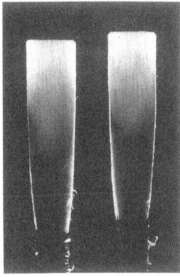

PLATE 1 The reeds of Jiri Tancibudek

David L. T. Woolley. Born August 30, 1924, in Shanghai, China, of Australian parents. At present Woolley is Co-principal Oboist, Royal Opera House, Covent Garden, London, England, where he has been since 1971. Other positions he has held include Cor Anglais in the Victoria Symphony Orchestra of Melbourne, Australia; Principal Oboist of the London Philharmonic Orchestra, 1955 and 1956; Principal Oboe, Sidney Symphony, Sidney, Australia, 1961–67; and Co-principal Oboe, Royal Philharmonic Orchestra, London, England, 1968–71. He is to be heard on commercial recordings of over one hundred orchestral works released by Decca, His Master's Voice, and Nixa. Woolley studied with Peter Newbury of London and plays a Rigoutat oboe with serial number 046 Z.

In 1958 Woolley gave the following measurements relative to his reeds: Pitch: A 440. Oboe staples: BL (designed by Brierly and manufactured by A. J. Lasenby of London, both deceased). Length of staple (Woolley's personal preference): 45 millimeters. Total length of reed: 71 millimeters. Thickness of gouge: .23 inches. Diameter of tube cane: 10 millimeters or 10.5 millimeters, depending on the density of the cane. Length of scrape: 12.5 millimeters. Quality of sound (in his opinion): fairly thick and lacking in buzz. Woolley considered the vital missing statistics to be the radius of the gouge blade and the angle at which it travels from horizontal, for which he lacked accurate measuring instruments. Woolley stated that a "school" of Australian oboe-playing had not yet developed, as Europeans and Europe-trained Australians have held positions only since the last war. Before World War II there were no permanent, full symphony orchestras. Now permanent orchestras are sponsored by the Australian Broadcasting Commission in six states.

In 1980 Woolley stated that he was using Glotin staples 47 millimeters in length and a Prestini shaper of No. 2 pattern. The overall length of the oboe reed is 75 millimeters with a V-scrape of 16–17 millimeters graduated toward the tip around a shaded central core.

Dates of information: 1958, 1980.

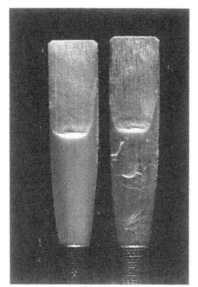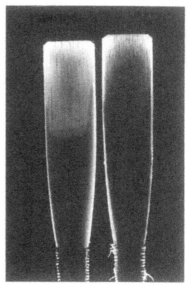

PLATE 2 The reeds of David L. T. Woolley

2. AUSTRIA (VIENNA)

Hans Kamesch. Born July 26, 1901, in Vienna, Austria. Deceased March 2, 1975. He became a member of the Staatsoper orchestra in Vienna, Austria, in 1922 under Richard Strauss and Franz -Schalk. From 1926 until 1958 he was Solo Oboe in the Staatsoper orchestra and the Vienna Philharmonic. Other positions he held include founding member of the Wind Ensemble of the Vienna Philharmonic (1928); Bayreuth Festival Orchestra and Salzburg Festival Orchestra, 1928–30; member of the Vienna Hofmusikkapelle, 1926–45; and teacher at the Staatsakademie für Musik, 1937–51. Kamesch was decorated by the king of Italy and honored by the president of Austria and the Vienna Philharmonic for his achievements as an oboist. In 1949 he premiered the Richard Strauss Oboe Concerto with the Vienna Philharmonic under Furtwängler. It was Kamesch who played Solo Oboe in *Fidelio* on the much-heralded opening after World War II of the Staatsoper in Vienna in 1955. Kamesch studied with Professors Baumgärtl and Wun-

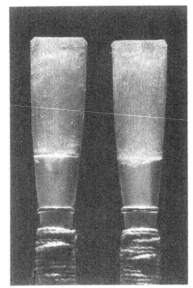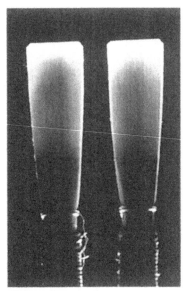

PLATE 3   The reeds of Hans Kamesch

derer at the Staatsakademie für Musik. He played a Viennese-style oboe made by Zuleger, No. 1017.

Kamesch stated in 1958 that he had been making reeds for about forty-one years. He made an average of two hundred reeds a year and finally performed on about twenty of them. He imposed the strict selection because of the tonal quality he wished to achieve. He also stated that most of the obvious, possibly surprising, differences between his own reeds and those of others stem from the Viennese "school" of playing.

For a photograph of Kamesch, see Plate XXXII in Baines, *Woodwind Instruments and Their History.*

Dates of information: 1958, 1980.

Manfred Kautzky. Born November 21, 1932, in Vienna, Austria. In 1958 Kautzky was an oboist in the Staatsoper orchestra in Vienna; in 1956 he went on the American tour with the Vienna Philharmonic. He was an oboist in the orchestra of the Volksoper in Vienna from 1958 until 1976. He joined the faculty of the Vienna

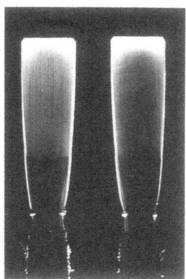

PLATE 4 The reeds of Manfred Kautzky

Hochschule für Musik in 1976 as Professor of Oboe. Kautzky studied with Kamesch and Hadamowsky. He plays a Zuleger oboe, No. 1023.
Dates of information: 1958, 1980.

André Lardrot. Born March 5, 1932, in Nevers, France. At present (1980) Lardrot is Solo Oboe of the Radio Symphony Orchestra of Basel, Switzerland, formerly the Orchestra of Radio-Zurich (transferred to Basel in 1970). He is also Professor of Oboe at the Conservatoire de Basel. In 1966 he was Solo Oboe in the Orchestra of Radio-Zurich and a professor at Hochschule Essen. Other positions he has held are First Solo Oboe of the Mozarteum Orchestra of Salzburg, Austria; First Solo Oboe, Radio Symphony Orchestra of Berlin; and Professor at the Akademie Mozarteum of Salzburg. Lardrot studied with Bajeux and Morel. In 1966 he played a Rigoutat oboe, No. 216 F. In 1980 he was playing Rigoutat oboe No. 284 HH.
Dates of information: 1966, 1980.

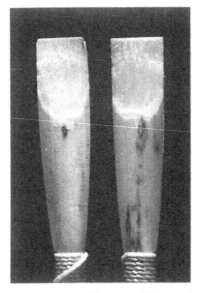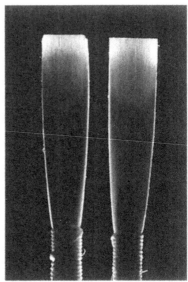

PLATE 5 The reeds of André Lardrot

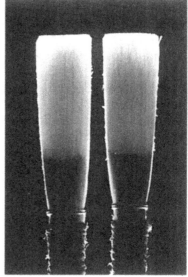

PLATE 6 The reeds of Ferdinand Raab

Ferdinand Raab. In 1958 Raab was a member of the 1st Oboe section of the Staatsoper orchestra in Vienna, Austria. He retired in 1977.
Dates of information: 1958, 1980.

3. CZECHOSLOVAKIA

Stanislav Duchoň. Born August 19, 1927, in Soboĉice, District of Kolín, Czechoslovakia. In 1958 Duchoň was the Principal Oboist of the Czech Philharmonic Orchestra. From 1948 to 1950 he played with the Prague City Orchestra, and from 1950 to 1957 he was a member of the Czech Broadcasting Orchestra. He attended the Prague Conservatory and the Prague Academy of Music, studying oboe with Professor Josef Děda and Professor František Hanták. Duchoň won First Prize at the Prague Spring Festival of 1955. In 1958 he was a member of a baroque chamber group, "Ars Rediviva." A frequent soloist, he has made several recordings, including the Mozart Quartet for Oboe and Strings. He plays a Cabart oboe with serial number DD 296 (1957).

Regarding his reeds, Duchoň states that he has practically no fixed measurements because he produces the reeds individually and tests them for pitch on the instrument with the aid of a tuning fork. He is not happy about his intonation, but he must make the entire reed a little shorter than he would like to because the Czech orchestras have a rather high pitch level. His reeds are based on those of Professor Josef Děda and several older colleagues, though he has added some of his own ideas based on his individual requirements.
Date of information: 1958.

František Hanták. Born June 19, 1910, in Lužnicí, Czechoslovakia. In 1958 Hanták was Solo Oboist of the State Philharmonic in Brno. After graduation from the State Conservatory at Prague, he played thirteen years in the Czech Philharmonic Orchestra and then joined the Symphony Orchestra of the Czech Broadcasting Company as Solo Oboist. He became a professor at the Academy of Musical Art in Prague upon its founding in 1946. From 1936 to 1956 he was a member of "Noneto," a chamber music group.

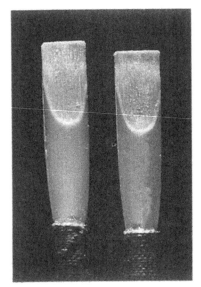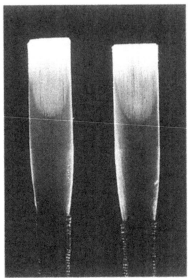

PLATE 7 The reeds of Stanislav Duchoň

Dedicated to solo playing for eighteen years, he was Solo Oboist of the State Philharmonic in Brno for two years, making twelve appearances in one year. Hanták was a guest artist with the Broadcasting Orchestra for a number of years after his regular employment with them and has recorded the Kramář-Krommer Concerto, opus 52, the Mozart C Major Concerto, the Handel G Minor Concerto, and the Cimarosa and Talich concerti.

Hanták tours throughout Europe as soloist and player with the Brno Philharmonic. He made appearances at the Brussels World's Fair and the fairs of Leipzig and Dresden, playing the Strauss Concerto at Dresden. He has been a guest with the Budapest Philharmonic and has played three solo concerts in Poland. Hanták has an extensive repertoire of solo and chamber music, and more than thirty pieces have been written especially for him.

In his travels through Europe, Hanták has made a collection of reeds from different countries and is of the opinion that judging reeds is a very personal matter because of differences in taste from one country to another. Recognizing the several schools of reed-

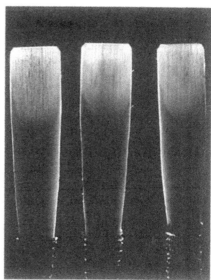

PLATE 8 The reeds of František Hanták

making in Europe, such as the French and German, he believes that the structure of the reed determines the tone quality. During his student years the German school of reedmaking was predominant in Czechoslovakia, but this style of reed, in his opinion, was rough and lacking in clarity. His professor, L. Skuhrovský, brought the Cabart oboe from France to Czechoslovakia, thus introducing the French reed. Because the French reed, having more clarity, was very different from the German, it was difficult at first for Hanták to adjust to it.

To point up the differences in taste between countries, he states that the tone of Eugene Goossens is not well accepted by the Czech public because the sound is foreign to their ears. Hanták himself admired the playing of Goossens, however. He feels that the French school is taking over in Europe where the German school left off, with the French having set out on the road to a greater tone.

During Hanták's youth in Czechoslovakia, only the piano, violin, cello, and voice were recognized in competitions. However, the oboe has now won its place in that country; after twenty-eight years of excellent solo playing, Hanták has no doubt been as responsible as anyone for this general acceptance.

Hanták teaches many private students and has carried on experiments with cane from China and other localities.

The three reeds that are represented in Plate 8 are chamber-music reeds, which have a softer tone than those which he prefers for orchestra concerts. Reeds that he plays in orchestra have a more nasal tone, while those he uses for solo work vary, as he matches the reed to the prevailing acoustics, the embouchure, and the music.

Date of information: 1958.

4. DENMARK

Waldemar Wolsing. Born May 3, 1910, in Hellerup, Denmark. He retired in 1970 as First Oboist of the Danish National Orchestra of the State Radio (Statsradiofoniens Symfoniorkester). From 1935 until 1940 he was oboist of the Tivoli Koncerthall Orchestra. Wolsing has studied with Svend Christian Felumb (1928–32), Henry Munck (1933–35), Louis Bleuzet (1932 and 1938), and Marcel Tabuteau (1950 and 1953 in France). He plays a Lorée oboe with serial number AQ 45.

Wolsing states that his conception of the ideal sound was achieved by Tabuteau; thus, in 1950 he changed from the school of Bleuzet to the school of Tabuteau. The left-hand reed in both photographs of Plate 9 is the reed that he used in playing for Columbia Recording 24/1-58. One of the pieces included on this recording is the Boisdeffre *Villanelle.* The right-hand reed is the one on which he played for the recording of the Tenth Symphony of Shostakovich and the Second Symphony of Borodin.

Wolsing remains active in the Union of Danish Musicians as well as several other musical groups and acts as consultant to the Danish Radio in musical matters.

Dates of information: 1958, 1980.

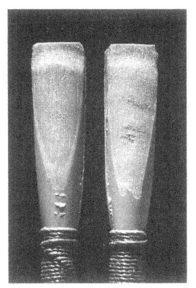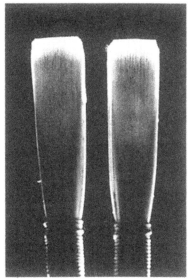

PLATE 9 The reeds of Waldemar Wolsing

5. ENGLAND

Harry B. Baker. Born 1912 in Maidstone, Kent, England. Baker has played oboe in the orchestra of the Royal Opera House, Covent Garden; the Royal Artillery Band, Woolwich, for sixteen years; with the Royal Philharmonic Orchestra, the BBC Symphony Orchestra, and many other orchestras, bands, and large and small chamber groups. He was a student of John Field's at the Royal Military School of Music, Kneller Hall, Twickenham, Middlesex, whence come a very large portion of the woodwind players in England. Baker plays a Louis oboe, serial number 409, ca. 1930. At the present time he is the proprietor of a reed manufacturing and music business in Welling, Kent. He makes reeds in many different styles, gouges to order, and scrapes to order for customers from many parts of the world.

Cane and Gouge. Baker's cane comes from southern Europe in bulk lots, and he finds that perhaps 25 percent of each shipment survives his selection process. He recognizes the following categories relative to the aural texture of cane: (1) bright texture—bright yellow cane (not deep yellow); hard, fine surface; smooth and silky feel; fine grain; (2) medium texture—fawn-color cane; a slightly oily feel; (3) dark texture—darker than fawn color; tends to be grainy. He further notes that mottling on the cane tends to mute the tone quality.

To ripen green cane, one should gouge first, then put the cane, inner part up, in a tray in the sun for varying periods of time, up to a half-day, depending upon the cane. Care should be taken not to leave it in the sun too long.

A wide shape is used, but it is trimmed at the sides to balance the other proportions. In general, the thicker the gouge, the longer the scrape; the thinner the gouge, the shorter the scrape. Also, the wider the reed, the shorter the scrape; the narrower the reed, the longer the scrape.

Staples: Baker uses 47-millimeter brass staples of his own manufacture. He feels that brass is more resonant and finds that when he uses a silver or copper (Prestini) staple, he must take more cane out of the center of the reed to let it vibrate. This adjustment is necessary because of the darker sound imparted by the less resonant staples.

Binding and Scraping: At present Baker is using 9-cord, reverse cable, satin-finish nylon thread for binding. It is slightly elastic and does not tend to loosen out. About three hundred reeds can be bound from a large reel.

After the cane is shaped and allowed to dry, about 8 millimeters of the open ends of the cane are soaked for about 30 seconds in hot water; then those ends are bound on the staple with the help of a hand drill with a mandrel in it. The bark is taken off very quickly with the use of an emery wheel mounted in a 3,000 rpm electric drill. Next, the upper half of the cane is soaked in hot water and the rest of the scrape is made with a scraping knife. The pitch, opening, and resistance are then adjusted in stages.

Baker follows the usual process of careful selection of tube cane, splitting the culms into three parts, putting those pieces through a filiere, and then gouging. The gouging machine is of a good, basic design incorporating four-way adjustment, and does an excellent job of gouging a few or hundreds of pieces of cane. Very simply, it is a wheel with a handle on it, which drives an eccentric circuit on the same axis. To the eccentric circle is joined a rod that runs through a series of bushings. Joined to the end of the rod, and before the last bushing, is the cutter assembly, on top of which is a handle for downward pressure. The wheel is turned with the right hand and the downward pressure on the blade-carrying slide is applied with the left. The bed is interchangeable, as is the cutter blade. The blade tends to work up on the forward stroke, leaving the cane thicker at the far end. Therefore, one must push down a bit harder on the blade as it approaches that end. The cutter is sharpened by eye, with care being taken to lighten the pressure over the center of the blade as it is rotated from side to side over the stone; otherwise, the center will wear twice as much as the sides. The cane is always gouged when dry.

Table 1 details the measurements Baker recommends, depending upon the character of the cane.

TABLE 1
Baker's Recommended Measurements

	Diameter of Tube Cane (mm.)	Gouge (in.)	Length of Scrape (mm.)	Overall Length (mm.)
Oboe				
Soft	10.5–11	.020–.021	6–7	69–70
Medium Soft	Same	.021–.022	8–9	71
Medium	Same	.022–.023	9–10	72
Oboe d'amore	11.5–12	.024	9–11	56 Med. Strength
Cor Anglais	12	.025	11–13	60 Med. Strength

This section has provided a short and admittedly oversimplified résumé of Baker's ideas of reedmaking, which have been formulated over many years of making reeds and playing double-reed instruments. His partner in the business is John Bessell (b. 1938, Hythe, Kent), formerly of the Royal Artillery Band. Bessell is now, in addition to his reedmaking, principally a free-lance art-

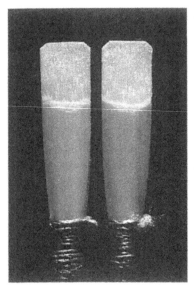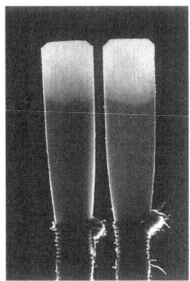

PLATE 10 The reeds of Harry B. Baker

ist in the London area and an oboe teacher. He has studied
with Steven Nye, Tom Danby, Janet Craxton, and Terence Mac-
Donagh. He plays Howarth oboe No. 1480.
Date of information: 1966.

Thomas Brierly (Brearley). Deceased 1952. Brierly lived in Liverpool and was extremely well known and highly respected as a
reedmaker. His reeds have had much influence on English oboe
playing over the last fifty years.
Date of information: 1958.

Janet Craxton. Born 1929 in London, England. Craxton started
her playing career in the Hallé Symphony Orchestra in 1949 and
then was a member of the BBC Symphony Orchestra for nine and
one-half years. She has been Principal Oboist of the London Sin-
fonietta since 1969 and Principal Oboist of the Royal Opera House
since 1979. She is a teacher at the Royal Academy of Music and,
as a free-lance artist, tours widely as a recitalist in England and

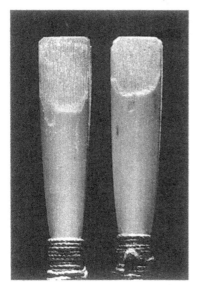
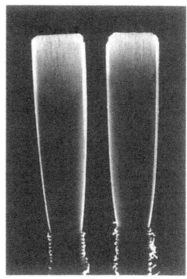

PLATE 11 The reeds of Thomas Brierly

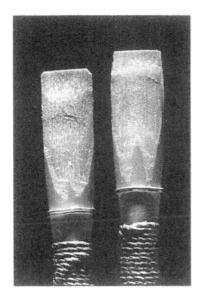
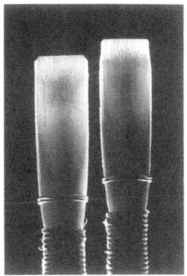

PLATE 12 The reeds of Janet Craxton

on the Continent. She studied with Helen Gaskell, P. Bajeux, and Whitney Tustin and plays Lorée oboe N 9 and a Lorée English horn.

Craxton gets Glotin tube cane and gouges it .55–.57 millimeters in the center. Her reeds are about 72–73 millimeters long when initially bound on the staple. Most of her reeds are on staples cut to 44–46 millimeters or shorter and are usually 68–70 millimeters overall.

Dates of information: 1968, 1980.

Peter Graeme. Born April 17, 1921, in Petersfield, England. He is Professor of Oboe at the Royal College of Music, a position he has held since 1949. He also shares the Principal Oboe position in the English Chamber Orchestra with Neil Black and plays in the Melos Ensemble. In 1974 he became a tutor at the Royal Northern College of Music, Manchester, England. Other positions he has held include oboist in the Philomusica of London and Second Oboe to Goossens in the London Philharmonic Orchestra in 1938–

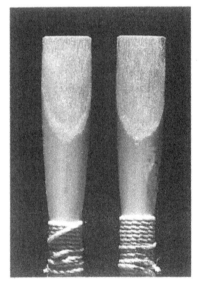

PLATE 13 The reeds of Peter Graeme

39. Graeme studied with Goossens and plays Louis oboe No. 411. In 1968 he was using reeds made by George Morgan, and he has also used reeds made by Otto Boden of Munich, Germany, for many years. He also tries reeds of other English makers from time to time and is experimenting with slightly thicker reeds with a W scrape.

Dates of information: 1968, 1980.

Tom Jones. Born December 7, 1906, in Ireland. Jones is now retired but held positions in the London Symphony Orchestra, the Old Vic, and the Royal Philharmonic Orchestra. He studied with Alec Whittaker and John Field. He plays a Louis oboe.

Jones gives the following measurements: a rather wide French shape, staples 1⅞ inch, 1 inch blade, and .023 inch thickness of gouge. The tube cane has a radius of 5.55 millimeters. See Table 3 for other measurements.

Date of information: 1968.

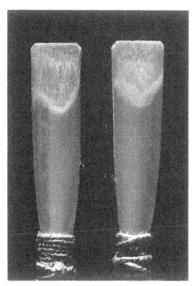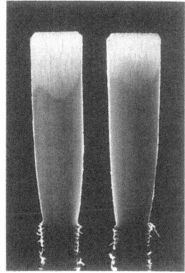

PLATE 14 The reeds of Tom Jones

Roger Lord. Born March 23, 1924, in Northallerton, Yorkshire. In 1967 he was Principal Oboe of the London Symphony Orchestra, a position he had held since 1952. Other positions Lord has held are Principal Oboe with both the BBC Midland Light Orchestra (1947–49) and the London Philharmonic Orchestra (1949–51). He studied with Terence MacDonagh and plays Boosey and Hawkes oboe No. 33126.

Lord remarks that he has played reeds made by T. Brierly, Tom Jones, and George Morgan and, of course, also makes his own. He states that the pitch nowadays seems to be going up, with the London Symphony Orchestra playing at about A 442 to 444, and that his oboe (1939) was built for a lower pitch. Consequently, as he likes a long blade, not too narrow, it becomes necessary to shorten the staples a little in order to get up to pitch, particularly on the low notes.

Date of information: 1967.

Terence MacDonagh, B.E.M., F.R.A.M., Hon. R.C.M. Born February 3, 1908, in London (Woolwich), England. MacDonagh's position in 1968 was that of Principal Oboist with the Royal Philharmonic Orchestra under Sir Thomas Beecham (now deceased). He has also played as guest Principal Oboist with the Philharmonic Orchestra, the London Symphony Orchestra, and other organizations. Until 1927 he played English horn with the BBC Symphony, then became Principal Oboist with that orchestra until 1939. From 1939 until 1945, he was in the British army as a member of the London Fire Service; he then rejoined the BBC Symphony until 1947. In 1947 he became a member of the Royal Philharmonic.

MacDonagh has studied with his father, J. A. MacDonagh; with Louis Bas and Mystil Morel, both in Paris; and with Leon Goossens. He plays a Howarth (London) oboe with serial number 1287.

The left-hand reed in both photographs of Plate 16, the older of the two reeds represented, was used for four performances of *Forza del Destino* at Glyndebourne last year. MacDonagh states that his reeds are now made by Tom Jones, who plays at the Old Vic Theatre in London, and that they give him the *ppppp* so

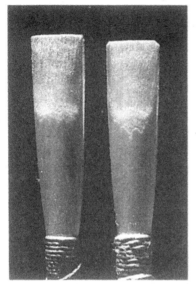
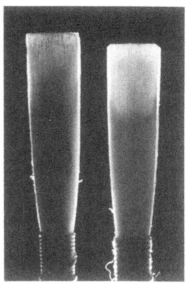

PLATE 15 The reeds of Roger Lord

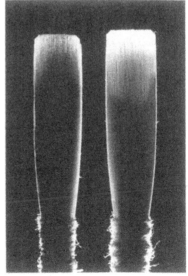

PLATE 16 The reeds of Terence MacDonagh

beloved by Sir Thomas Beecham. He has at other times used reeds made by Harry Baker and Harry Mier.

Date of information: 1968.

Peter Newbury. Born March 19, 1914, in Redditch, Worcestershire, England. In 1968 Newbury was Principal Oboist with the BBC Light Music Section and English horn player of the Philharmonia Orchestra, also playing the English horn for the London Philharmonic Orchestra from 1938 to 1940. For three years he was Principal Oboist and the English horn player with the Royal Philharmonic Orchestra. Newbury studied with J. A. MacDonagh, the father of Terence MacDonagh, and H. Halstead. He plays a Louis (London) oboe with serial number 719.

Regarding the technical details of his reeds, Newbury states,

> I gouge my cane to a thickness of .022 of an inch in the centre and .027 of an inch on the ends. They have a rather marked taper from the centre toward each end of the cane. The diameter of the cane is 10 mm., but in very warm weather I use 10.5 mm. cane. I could manage with 10.5 mm. cane all the time if I had to. The radius of the inside of the cane when gouged is 15/16 of an inch to 7/32 of an inch—it varies slightly, of course, unless the diameter of the cane is constant. The finished reed is 7 mm. wide, but I usually have to make it slightly more narrow after scraping in order to make it blow freely.

Date of information: 1968.

Evelyn Rothwell (Lady Evelyn Barbirolli). Born January 24, 1911, in Wallingford, England. She is a soloist, chamber music player, and recording artist of international fame. Lady Barbirolli has not accepted any orchestral work since her marriage in 1939. From 1931 until 1939 she held positions with the Glyndebourne Festival Opera Orchestra, the London Symphony Orchestra, the Queens Hall Orchestra, the Busch Chamber Music Players and many other musical organizations. She studied with Leon Goossens and plays a Howarth (London) oboe with serial number 1244.

Lady Barbirolli gouges her own cane from the tube, preferring to make her reeds herself from the beginning. Sometimes, when she is allowing the poorer quality tube cane to mature, she uses

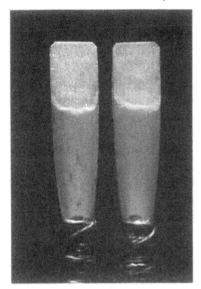
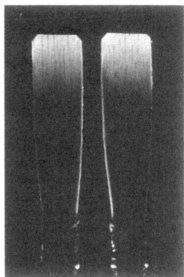

PLATE 17 The reeds of Peter Newbury

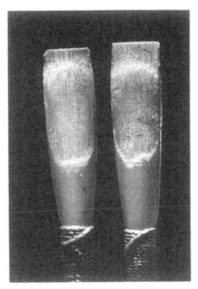
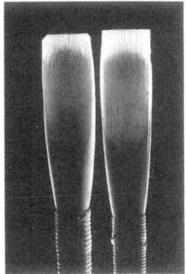

PLATE 18 The reeds of Evelyn Rothwell

gouged and shaped cane from Le Jolif of Lille, France (she finds his gouging and shaping just like her own). She states, "It is my honest opinion that the two most important factors in making a good reed are (a) the quality of the cane, and (b) the radius and setting of the gouge blade. Fine shaping and scraping are vital also, but I feel that the gouging is enormously important." Date of information: 1960.

Sidney Sutcliffe. Born 1918 in Edinburgh, Scotland. He was in the King's Royal Rifle Corps Band in 1934 and in 1935 accepted a Kneller Hall Scholarship. He has played under all major conductors and has been a member of the Sadler's Wells Ballet Orchestra. Sutcliffe was a member of the London Philharmonic Orchestra, leaving to join the BBC Symphony Orchestra as Principal Oboist. He studied with William Shepley and Leon Goossens and plays a Boosey and Hawkes oboe with serial number 32038.

Sutcliffe prefers a gouge of .60 millimeters for his Boosey and Hawkes oboe, which is a rather free-blowing instrument. His Louis oboe offers more resistance, and he therefore prefers a gouge of .58 millimeters for reeds to be used with that instrument. He made reeds in the style of T. Brierly at one time, and now, even though he does not make a short scrape reed, he still holds to many of Brierly's basic principles, such as gouging dry on a muggy day and matching the gouge to the cane (e.g., stiff, hard cane should be gouged thinner than soft cane). Date of information: 1968.

William H. Tait. Born August 24, 1890, in Birmingham, England. One of three woodwind players who founded the Harrow Symphony Orchestra in 1939, Tait played oboe in that orchestra for many years thereafter. He also played bassoon, violin, and viola in the orchestra. He studied oboe with Sylvia Spencer (a student of Leon Goossens) and reedmaking with Evelyn Rothwell and Thomas Brierly. He plays Louis oboe No. 455 and an English horn by Lorée.

Tait is a distinguished metallurgical and mechanical engineer and in 1968 was very active as a highly respected engineering consultant. Over the years, in addition to his engineering work,

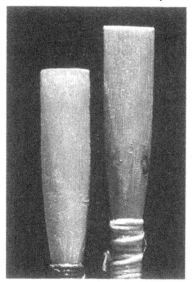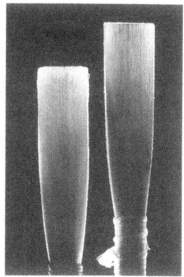

PLATE 19 The reeds of Sidney Sutcliffe

he has applied his scientific mind to an investigation of the factors inherent in the overall acoustical systems of the oboe and bassoon. He has a workshop in his home and has made many improvements on the gouging machine, profiler, electroforming of staples, etc.

Figure 17 shows two views of a Tait-designed gouge cutter blade that keeps its shape automatically when sharpened. Figure 18 shows the way in which the cutter blade is mounted in the machine. The cutter is a slice of round, "silver steel" (1 percent carbon) rod cut at an angle of 30° and hardened and tempered in the usual way. The angled face provides the correctly curved cutting edge, and the blade requires stoning only on the flat face to sharpen. The cutter is hollowed out, as shown by the dotted lines, to reduce the area that has to be stoned. By altering one angle, as by a wedge-shaped packing piece behind the blade, one can vary the amount the gouged cane thins toward the edges; the more nearly upright the tool back, the more nearly the thickness at the edges approximates the thickness at the center of the gouge. The diameter of the steel rod from which the cutter is made should be approximately the same as the diameter of the bed of

the machine. On Tait's machine both of these dimensions are
½ inch.

The sliding part of the gouger (the rounded part that has the
cutting blade part-way along it) is made much longer than usual
so that part of it presses on the cane at all times, thus preventing
the cane from jumping out and eliminating the common flip-over
restraining pieces at the ends of the conventional gouge bed.
Tait puts a smear of light oil on the inner surface of the cane
before starting to gouge. He prefers a gouge of approximately
.0215 inches in the center, tapering to .015 inches on the edges,
depending upon the cane. A final scrape with a disc-type scraper
on the gouged side of the cane makes it possible to have a cleaner
tip to the finished reed by doing away with the unanchored ends
of cane fiber.

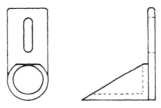

FIG. 17 Tait gouge blade. *Left*, end view;
right, side view.

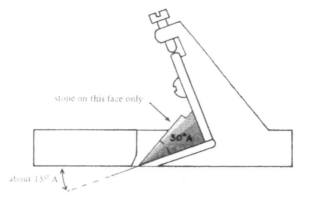

FIG. 18 Carrier assembly with mounted
gouge blade

The following is Tait's translation of part of the chapter dealing with reeds from A. Bridet's *L'education du Hautboiste*. Figure 19 is Tait's diagram of Bridet's suggested dimensions for gouged cane.

The oboe reed calls for a cane with a diameter between 10.5 and 11.0 mms.; the oboe d'amore from 11 to 11.5 mms.; the cor anglais from 11.5 to 12 mms.; the bass oboe from 13 to 14 mms. [For comparison, he gives 22 mm. for the bassoon and 25 mm. for the contra bassoon.]

The cane, as in the time of the Greeks, must not be used until three years after it has been cut. It must be chosen with scrupulous care, the tubes having the correct diameter and the wood being adequately dense. The tubes are cut into the necessary lengths and then split into three segments; each split section is then brought to a convenient thickness by passing it through the "rough sizing gouge" [free translation of "filiere," assuming he means the conventional fixed gouge in a part cylindrical bed, where the split cane is pushed under the gouge, along the bed].

The cane, which has preferably been soaking in water for an hour or two to soften it, is next gouged. It is during this operation that the cane can be finally selected. You can tell a good cane by its clear translucence; healthy and vigorous appearance; even grain.

The gouged cane, with its naturally cylindrical outer face, should now in cross section present the appearance of a crescent. The attached diagram shows this section enlarged ten times, the measurements being those for cane 11 mm. diameter. For larger cane, dimensions will be proportionately larger. Note that the thickness at the middle is 1/20 the diameter so that with cane 11 mm. diameter this figure is 11/20 mm. [say .022"]. Never gouge thinner than this, and do not exceed it by more than one or two twentieths of a millimetre [say plus .002 or .004"].

The thickness at the edge of the cane varies according to the centre that you choose for striking the inner, the gouged, circle. It can vary between .2 and .6 mm. [The centres for .25 and .4 mms. are shown at C^1 and C^2 on fig. 19.] This edge thickness has a powerful influence on the tone of the instrument. Thin edges give a tone that is always rather dry and weak on the high notes and upper partials. Thicker edges on the other hand make for warmth of tone, particularly in the higher notes. Everyone must choose thickness that best suits him, and his instrument.

Half way along the gouged cane is now lightly nicked so that it can be bent in two onto the "shape" ["taille anche," "gabarit"]. With the "shape" the cane is brought to the desired profile and appears as two tongues which are securely bound to the staple. This staple influences the tone and intonation of the instrument; conical in shape, it must match the bore of the instrument.

To help them vibrate the double reeds are now scraped with a knife—taking care to scrape both blades identically. Length of scrape is also proportioned to the thickness of the cane. Thus, reeds gouged so as to be 11/20 mm. at the centre will have a scrape 11 mm. long. A uniform scrape yields a uniform graduation in translucence and leaves the base of the scrape curved like the base of a fingernail where the untouched skin of the cane meets the scrape.

A well-scraped reed has several millimetres near the tip very clear and uniformly tapered. It is most important to avoid a curved scrape, leading to an arched cross section like a V or a U. This only leads to a nasal quality of tone and provokes "quacks" [French "couacs"]. No, the scrape must be even with uniform taper.

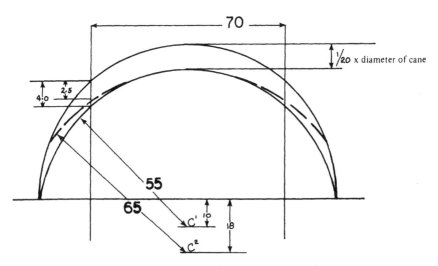

Fig. 19 Section of gouged oboe cane × 10 in mms.

Staples: Tait makes his staples by electrodeposition with a thickness of 0.8 to 0.9 millimeters for brass staples and about 0.11 millimeters for copper ones. The standard length is 47 millimeters. The measurement of the staple bore (large end) is 0.187 inches, the top of the oboe bore 0.140 inches, and the oboe socket 0.250 inches. He mentions that cutting off about $\frac{3}{16}$ of an inch of the staple and pulling the reed out to play in tune (leaving the stepped cavity between the end of the staple and the oboe bore) much improves the tone quality on his Louis oboe. This technique was, of course, not possible to such a great extent on the early reverse taper oboes, into which was inserted the waxed-thread lapped staple.

In experiments with staples that were true extensions of the oboe bore (no inward "step" from the larger staple opening to the smaller oboe bore), he found that the top notes were not possible to play. Also, staples that flare to nearly the bore of the socket are equally unsatisfactory. These experiments lead us to suppose that the present staple arose naturally, and it seems very difficult to improve on it.

Shape: The following measurements indicate Tait's shaper widths at 3-millimeter intervals from staple end.

> 3.60 mm.
> 4.30
> 4.95
> 5.55
> 6.10
> 6.50
> 6.75
> 7.0 Parallel from this point.

Cane: Tait gets cane from Fréjus and states that the modulus of elasticity of his best cane was as high as 1,500,000 pounds/square inch in the lengthwise direction, but only 60,000 pounds/square inch across the grain.

Tait gives the following account of the growing and harvesting of French cane:

The plant used for woodwind reeds is known to botanists as *Arundo Donax*, and, though it is fairly widely distributed through-

out the world, only those from three small districts in the south
of France seem capable of producing reeds that will give a good
tone. These places are Fréjus, Cogolin and Hyeres. I have visited
the first two which are in flat, alluvial valleys two or three miles
broad, between hills rising to some 2,000 feet. The main crop of
both regions is the grape vine, though a lot of fruit is also grown.
Both valleys are intersected by numerous streams and irrigation
ditches which, in winter, carry the water from the hills to the
main river of each valley. In summer they are dry. The reeds, or
roseaux, as they are called locally, grow on the banks of these
streams, and serve a double purpose, for they both protect the vines
from the mistral, a bitterly cold wind which blows at intervals
during the winter, and also form a useful secondary crop for the
owner of the vineyard.

The *roseaux* belong to the grass family, and they may be likened
to huge pieces of grass, about 18 feet high, with a woody stem.
They are cut down when two years old, in February or March,
tied into bundles, and piled into stacks rather like wigwams, so
that the air can circulate among the canes. Here they dry for a
little over a year.

In the following spring they are taken down and sorted. Some
become fishing rods, some garden canes, and some are split length-
ways and made into sun-blinds resembling miniature chestnut
palings. Only the straightest parts of the cane are kept for instrument reeds and these, cut into lengths of about four feet, are laid
on racks in the hot summer sun. They are turned over every eve-
ning, and at the end of a week, they have ripened from a muddy
brown to a rich golden yellow colour.

Finally, they are cut into the pieces or tubes, about eight or ten
inches long, in which they reach the reed-maker. They are sorted
into their different instruments according to their diameter, the
thickest, a little more than an inch in diameter, being for saxo-
phones and bass clarinets. Then come the pieces for clarinet and
bassoon reeds. The thinnest of all, about only a quarter of an
inch thick, are used for oboes. Many sacks of cane are also sent
from the Department of Var to Scotland and Ireland to become
bagpipe reeds.

The pre-eminence of the French reeds is recognized fairly generally among woodwind players, though so far I have not heard
of any well-authenticated reason for this excellence. M. Pleven,
the doyen of the Fréjus *roseurs*, says it is due to the presence of

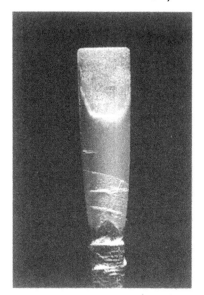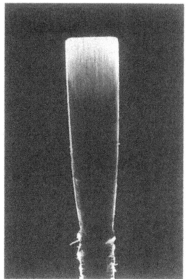

PLATE 20 A reed of William Tait

aluminum in the soil, which is a very reasonable suggestion. However, it is probably not quite as simple as that, and it is more
likely to be the combined effect of the long, dry summer, the
abundant water only a few feet below ground level throughout
the year, and the chemical composition of the soil. It would be
hard to find another region where all three factors unite to produce an exactly similar result, and this would explain the lack of
success which has, so far, been the fate of all who have tried to
grow satisfactory reed-cane in this country.

Date of information: 1968.

Derek Wickens. Born June 25, 1937, in Hyth, Kent, England. He
is presently Principal Oboe in the Royal Philharmonic Orchestra.
For a two-year period starting in 1968 he was Solo Oboe at the
Royal Opera House, Covent Garden, under Solti. Other positions
he has held include Second Oboe in the Royal Liverpool Philharmonic Orchestra (1960–63) and Principal Oboe at Sadler's
Wells Opera House (1963–64). Wickens is a founding member of
the Tuckwell Wind Quintet, which was formed in 1969. A re-

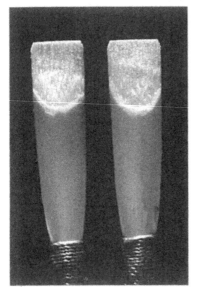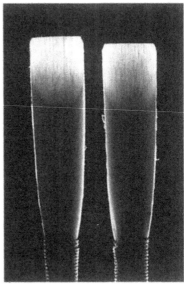

Plate 21 The reeds of Derek Wickens

cording by the quintet and also one of Wickens playing the Marcello, Haydn, and Albinoni A Minor Concertos is scheduled for release in 1981. Wickens studied with Anthony Danby and Terence MacDonagh and plays Howarth oboe No. 1379.

Wickens makes the following remarks:

> I gouge 10.5 mm. cane to .022″ with fairly thick sides. I gouge the cane dry, and just before the first strokes of gouging I apply a small drop of oil to the cane. I find that this lengthens the life of the blade. This method was recommended to me by Mr. L. E. Winfield, who made my gouging machine. I leave the gouged cane at least 24 hours, and then soak in cold water for 30 minutes before shaping. My shape is also made by Winfield to my specifications, which I think is fairly standard over here. I then tie the cane on immediately, rough scrape them and leave for a further 24 hours before completing.

Dates of information: 1968, 1980.

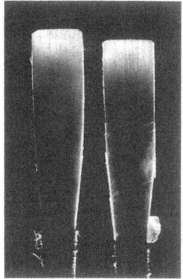

PLATE 22 The reeds of Asser Sipila

6. FINLAND

Asser Sipila. Mr. Sipila was the Solo Oboist of the Symphony Orchestra of Helsinki, Finland, in 1958.

7. FRANCE

Pierre Bajeux. (Deceased.) In 1958 M. Bajeux was Professor of Oboe at the Paris Conservatoire and a colleague of Claro's in the Opéra orchestra.

L. F. A. Bleuzet (1874–1961) followed Georges Gillet as Professor of Oboe at the Paris Conservatory in 1929. He had considerable influence in France, both as a teacher and a player. He was also First Oboist of the Concerts du Conservatoire and of the Opéra.

For this example of Bleuzet's reed, supplied in 1958, the writer is indebted to Waldemar Wolsing, First Oboist of the Danish National Orchestra of the State Radio, who studied with Bleuzet.

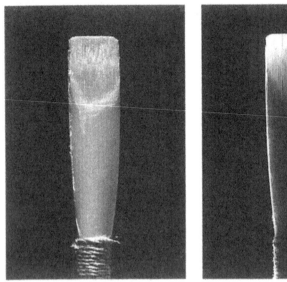
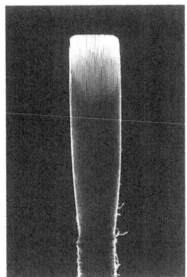

PLATE 23 A reed of Pierre Bajeux

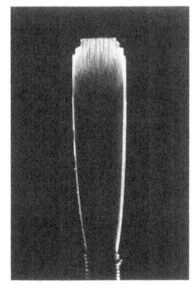

PLATE 24 A reed of L. F. A. Bleuzet

André Chevalet. Born February 17, 1923, in Savières (Aube), France. He joined the Orchestre Philharmonique de l'O.R.T.F. as Solo Oboe in 1948 and has held that position for the last thirty-two years. In 1975 the name of that orchestra was changed to Nouvel Orchestre Philharmonique de Radio France. Other positions he has held include Oboe and Cor Anglais with the Orchestre des Concerts Pasdeloup and the Orchestre de Musique de Chambre Oubradous. Chevalet is a winner of the first prize for oboe of the Conservatoire National de Musique and was a prize winner at the International Concours de Musique, Geneva, 1946. He studied with Bleuzet, Gromer, and Bajeux, all of the Conservatoire. He plays a Rigoutat oboe.

Chevalet believes that the tone quality of the reed can usually be improved by making the reed "just so," and that amateurs and professionals alike are constantly preoccupied with this question, even within their own individual tonal concepts.

He notes that one should avoid a vibrato that has an ugly speed; the musical phrase should always be in evidence; the tone should be beautiful and ringing—round, warm, and clear—not pale or without life, or the opposite—harsh or aggressive.

The scrape, shape, and thickness of the cane, and above all its tonal qualities, give different results, and more or less fit the artist's embouchure. Thus, it is up to the artist to adopt principles of improvement and adjustment that are suited to him without going off too far from the established method. After all, it is the results that count.

The method that he has adopted (because it suits him) is to make a very thin and short tip and to leave much of the wood at the place where it must rest upon the lips. Thus, it is easy to play octaves, and one can "push" the scrape until one is able to play the low notes.

His reeds are cut from canes 10.5 to 11 millimeters in diameter. The gouge is 0.55 to 0.60 millimeters thick in the center, and 0.40 to 0.45 millimeters on the sides. The length of the staple is 47 millimeters, width of shape 7 millimeters, and overall length 72 millimeters.

Dates of information· 1966, 1980.

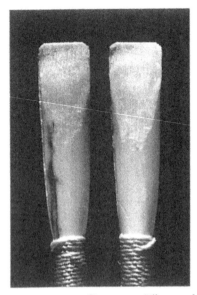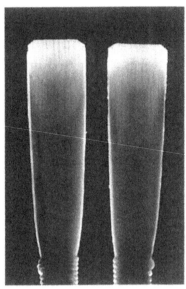

PLATE 25   The reeds of André Chevalet

Raymond Claro. Born September 4, 1910, in Cambrai (Nord), France. Claro is now retired from the Théâtre National de l'Opéra, Paris, France, in which he held a position from 1942 until 1971. Other positions he has held include those in the Radio Paris, which he joined in 1932, and Radiodiffusion Nationale, which he joined in 1937. He studied with Bleuzet and plays a Rigoutat oboe.
Dates of information: 1958, 1980.

8. GERMANY

Helmut Eggers. Born December 1, 1913, in Hamburg, Germany. In 1958 Eggers was Solo Oboist of the Symphony Orchestra of Radio Hamburg. He studied with Albert Reinhard of the Hamburg Philharmonic Orchestra. He plays an oboe made by Gustav Urban of Hamburg.

Fritz Fischer. Born September 17, 1910, in Klingenthal, Germany. In 1958 Fischer was Solo Oboist of the Symphony Orchestra of

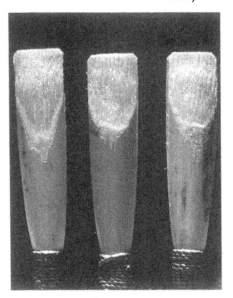

PLATE 26 The reeds of Raymond Claro

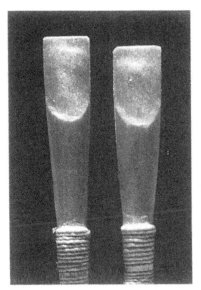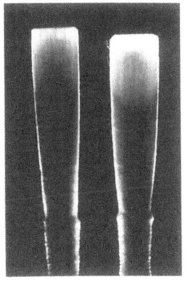

PLATE 27 The reeds of Helmut Eggers

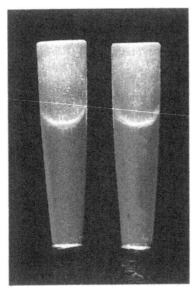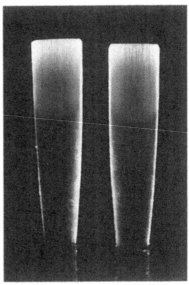

PLATE 28 The reeds of Fritz Fischer

Radio-Stuttgart, Stuttgart, Germany. He studied with Professors König and Geisler, both of Dresden. Fischer plays a Mönnig (Markneukirchen) oboe, No. 5028.

Regarding his reeds, Fischer states he has experimented for many years with reed cane from many countries. For the past twenty years, however, he has used cane grown in Spain. He explains that not every harvest turns out equally well, naturally, but on the average, he feels Spanish cane is the best.

Date of information: 1958.

Kurt Kalmus. In 1958 Kalmus was First Oboe of the Bavarian Radio Orchestra, Munich, Germany.

Helmut Schlövogt. Born September 19, 1911, in Leipzig, Germany. He was Solo Oboist of the Gewandhaus Orchester, Leipzig, from 1933 until 1941; oboe teacher at the Hochschule für Musik, Leipzig, from 1934 until 1941; Solo Oboist of the Berliner Philharmonic, Berlin, from 1941 until 1974; and oboe teacher of the

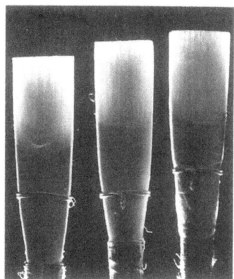

PLATE 29 The reeds of Kurt Kalmus

Internationalen Musikinstitut, Berlin, from 1946 until 1950. Schlövogt is now retired from the Berliner Philharmonic and is teaching at the professional school in Altötting, South Bavaria.

Schlövogt was a student at the Hochschule für Musik in Leipzig, where he studied oboe with Alfred Gleissberg, from 1928 until 1933. Over his years as a professional musician he has played oboes of Otto Mönnig, Leipzig, with serial numbers 7482 and 7641; Marigaux oboe number 1167; and, since 1972, Rigoutat oboe o80 EE. He has recommended Noblet oboes for many of his present students.

Schlövogt states that in his early years of playing he always got cane from Rinkel-Girard, Fréjus, France. He became unhappy with the cane from southern France because the cane plantations were no longer curing cane very well. He then experimented with the synthetic material "PVC" for many years and found that he could make reeds for nonsolo tasks out of this material. He has given up this experimentation because there has been some recent publicity regarding the possibility that "PVC" may be a health

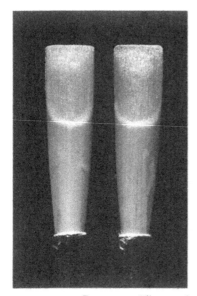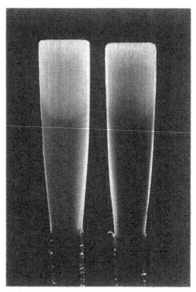

PLATE 30   The reeds of Helmut Schlövogt

hazard. Schlövogt uses a gouging machine from the firm of Krause, Kunde, and Sassenberg. He selects tube cane with a diameter of 9–10 millimeters in the center, tapering to .040 millimeters on the sides.

Dates of information: 1968, 1980.

Herman Töttcher. Born December 16, 1909, in Hannover, Germany. Deceased 1959. In 1958 he was Solo Oboist in the Radio-Sinfonie Orchester, Berlin, Germany. He had held previous orchestral positions in Frankfurt and Düsseldorf. Töttcher studied with Louis Bleuzet in Paris and played oboes by Mönnig (Markneukirchen), Nos. 384 and 560.

Töttcher remarked that the two examples of reeds presented here did not quite have the length that he preferred because the tuning of the orchestra was very high. But he used this length because of the better stability in the medium and low registers and in the diminuendo and *pp*. Also, there was less sagging of the lower notes, a condition that sometimes exists when reeds are too long.

The quality of the cane, its resilience, curvature, and absorbability are most important. Also very important is the quality of regeneration of the reed blades, i.e., an inner resilience and strength to open themselves again. The elasticity brought on by this natural resilience is particularly effective in staccato. Staccato is much less effective on a reed with a flat or nonelastic opening. A reed with a good opening gives greater security and also makes possible a greater dynamic range and a larger tone, which can be used in the service of the musical feeling of the player.

The manner of scraping has great influence on the quality and fullness of sound.

Each player imagines the quality of tone, the desired quality of the timbre, and the range and flexibility of expression quite individually. A reed will be made in an individual manner, according to the player's concept. Thus, there are three important components of a superb overall (musical) effort: (1) the talent of the player as a natural artist; (2) an instrument that yields its own excellent timbre and is brought to life by the player; and (3) the reed in its optimal condition.

In regard to point (1), Töttcher quoted Schumann (freely translated): "Whoever does not play with the instrument does not play it." There must be great technical and breath control over, and as one with, the instrument—a complete coupling of the breath and the instrument that makes it possible for the player to launch an attack that overcomes the natural resistances of the reed and the instrument.

One should not place the reed too far into the mouth as doing so restricts the overtone series from sounding with equal intensity over the range. If that occurs, the basic tone takes the brightness from the tonal color and the tone consequently sounds like that of a clarinet or a low flute. This is not in character for an instrument that was originally considered a light, high-tone instrument among the other wind instruments, the "violin" of the woodwinds of former times. For the French school this characteristic has never changed, and the concert literature of the eighteenth century demands this lightness of tone combined with the sound of string instruments and cembalo. Töttcher played a true baroque oboe from Buchsbaum and it had the high silvery tone that was praised by the critics of the time.

With regard to the embouchure, the reed should not be pressed tightly between the lips, but should be held in such a manner as to allow for the varying air pressure and air speed in the different registers.

The thickness of the gouge has great influence on the stability of the tone in all registers. A thickness less than .50 millimeters is too thin and causes unstable and shaky sounds, and the high register sounds very thin. His best experience was with cane gouged .55 millimeters, but a gouge of .60 millimeters in thickness gives greater stability to tone quality and attack, especially in the high register.

The following eighteenth-century oboe concerti and sonatas were edited by Töttcher and published by Hans Sikorski, Hamburg 13:

Concerti: J. S. Bach, Oboe Concerto in F Major; Telemann, Concerti in D Minor, E Minor; Stölzel, Concerto in C Major; Johann Stamitz, Concerto in C Major.

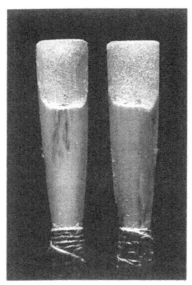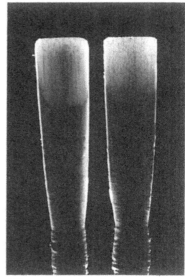

PLATE 31   The reeds of Hermann Töttcher

Sonatas: Kirnberger, Telemann (both with cembalo and basso continuo).

Töttcher recorded the following for Archive Production of DGG: 3 Concerti of Handel (played on the Buchsbaum oboe); 1 Concerto of Johann Stamitz; 2 Quartets of Telemann; Telemann, Concerto for 3 Oboes, 3 Violins, Basso Continuo; Telemann, Concerto for Flute, Oboe d'amore, Viola d'amore, Strings and Basso Continuo; Mozart, Quintet K. 452 (played on the Buchsbaum oboe).

Dates of information: 1958, 1980.

9. HOLLAND

Simon Houttuin. Born January 3, 1924, in Amsterdam, Holland. In 1958 Houttuin was Solo Oboist of the Rotterdam Philharmonic Orchestra and teacher at the Rotterdam Conservatory. He also played in the orchestra of the Netherlands Opera. He studied with W. Peddemors of Amsterdam and played an open-holed Püchner oboe.

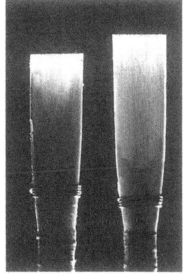

PLATE 32 The reeds of Simon Houttuin

Houttuin states that when playing he pulls the rather short staples out about $\frac{1}{12}$ of an inch to $\frac{1}{8}$ of an inch. He plays at a pitch level of A 442 cps.

Date of information: 1958.

Ferdinand Maria Hubertus Pels. Born August 29, 1887, in The Hague, Netherlands. Pels is retired as First Oboist of the Utrecht Municipal Orchestra and as teacher at the Utrecht Conservatory of Music. Other oboe positions he has held include those in the Comic Opera of Berlin, the French Opera of The Hague, and the Kur Orchestra of Scheveningen. He studied with H. de Witt of the Royal Conservatory in The Hague and plays a Cabart oboe with serial number H 74.

Pels states that at the beginning of his career he used oboes made by Heckel, a German maker, but changed to French oboes in 1907. He did not study the special methods of various composers such as Sellner, Besfoci, Ferling, Brod, Verroust, and Barret. At first he chiseled [gouged] cane by hand; later he switched to machine.

Date of information: 1958.

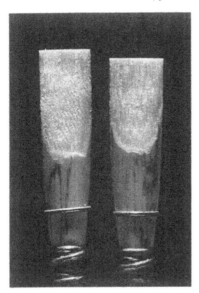 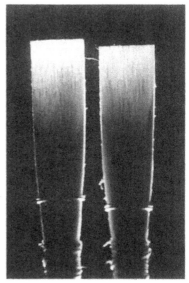

PLATE 33 The reeds of Ferdinand Pels

Jaap Stotijn. Born September 22, 1891, in The Hague, Netherlands. Stotijn retired in 1956 as a teacher of the Royal Conservatory of Music, The Hague, and as Solo Oboist of the Residence Orchestra of The Hague. He had been associated with both of these institutions for forty-one years. In 1959 Stotijn still played regularly and taught twenty-five students at that time. He recorded the Mozart Quartet, K.V. 370, for Philips. A recording of the Mozart Concerto in C Major (Boosey and Hawkes edition) with Stotijn as soloist with the Vienna Philharmonic, directed by Wilhelm Leibner, has also been released by Philips.

Stotijn held conducting positions with the Royal Orchestra Society "Symphonia of Rotterdam" for ten years, the Students' Orchestra "Apollo" of Delft for twelve years, and the Students' Orchestra "Sempre Crescendo" of Leiden for twelve years.

While studying oboe with Dirk van Emmerik, Stotijn played for four years in the Residence Orchestra while van Emmerik was First Oboist. He still considers van Emmerik the best oboist who ever lived. Stotijn himself won the Silver Fock-Medallion for oboe playing and a certificate for solo and orchestra playing. An excellent pianist as well as a famous oboist, he studied piano with Everhard van Beijnum and received a teaching certificate from the Royal Conservatory of Music. He studied violin with his eldest brother, Constant Stotijn. He plays a Lorée oboe with serial number AE 60.

Stotijn makes the following remarks about his reeds:

I make reeds somewhat wider and thicker than French reeds. As a consequence, I make the tubes [*stiften*] and both sides somewhat shorter—about 2 mm. on the upper side and about 5 mm. on the bottom. Therefore, the diapason is higher and I do not have to strain, but can blow with a loose embouchure. The shorter tube makes the tone clearer, and because of the wider and thicker reed, I get more "trilling" and more ease in high and low tones. Because the reed is thicker, I also can put on the little copper band, which is impossible for the French oboists. Consequently, the sides cannot slip over each other; when the reed is opened up, I can close it more with the copper band, and conversely, when the reed is closed, I can open it up again. Another important matter is that I never have to strain because the little band is doing part of the work that otherwise would be performed by the lips.

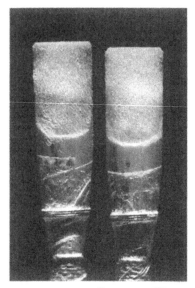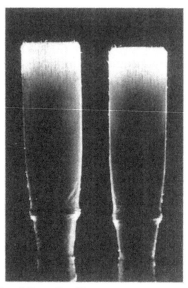

PLATE 34 The reeds of Jaap Stotijn

You can further see distinctly that the reed blades have two "mirrors." The surface of these is very equal and smooth, and, therefore, the reeds easily reach the low and high tones.

Date of information: 1959.

10. ITALY

Tullio Riedmiller. Born June 13, 1892, in Trento, Italy. In 1959 Riedmiller had been Professor of Oboe at the State Conservatory of Music "Benedetto Marcello" of Venice for forty years and was Solo Oboist of the theater "La Fenice di Venezia." He studied with Giuseppe Prestini, first in Venice and later at the State Conservatory "Cherubini" in Florence. Riedmiller played an oboe made by Romeo Orsi, Via Luretti 46, Milano, Italy.

Reidmiller has had a distinguished teaching career, counting among his more famous students Professor Italo Toppo of the State Conservatory of Torino; Professor Angelo Bergamaschi of the State Conservatory of Trieste; Professor Aldo Girardello, who

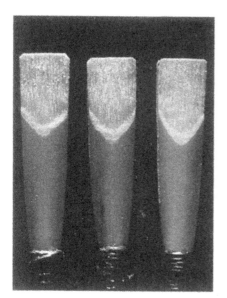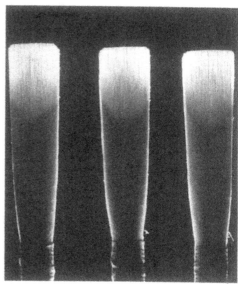

PLATE 35 The reeds of Tullio Riedmiller

formerly taught in Shanghai, China, played in the Shanghai Symphony, and is now in Venezuela; Professor Alberto Caroldi of Mexico City, who formerly was Solo Oboist of the Radio Orchestra of Milano; Professor Wolf-Ferrari, English-horn player of the Santa Cecilia Orchestra of Rome; and Professor Wladimiro Cambruzzi, English-horn player and Reidmiller's substitute at the "Teatro La Fenice" in Venice.

Reidmiller's reeds, of the style of Lorée, are made by Professor Romeo Orsi of Milano, Italy. He prefers these reeds for their tone quality and because the low notes are well in tune. For the reed to be in tune, the staples must be 46.5 millimeters long and the finished reed 72 millimeters long. The gouge of the cane is .55 millimeters. The length of scrape is 7.5 millimeters.

Date of information: 1959.

Fedorico de Sanctis. Born April 23, 1910, in Florence, Italy. In 1959 de Sanctis was Solo Oboist of the Orchestra del Maggio Musicale Fiorentino as well as teacher and conductor of the or-

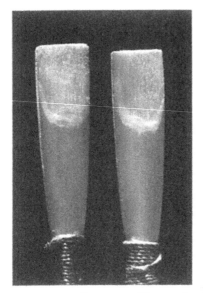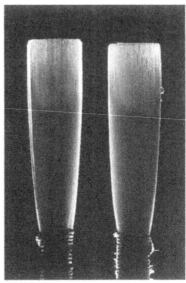

PLATE 36 The reeds of Federico de Sanctis

chestra at the Conservatory of Music "Luigi Cherubini" in Florence. He studied oboe with Giuseppe Prestini, the head of the
Italian school of oboe playing. De Sanctis played an oboe of the
French Conservatory type 6 B, with keys that he and Prestini
added. His instrument was made by Spartaco Incagnoli of Rome.
He is a well-known conductor, especially in Europe, where he
has toured extensively as an opera conductor. He has also appeared
as oboe soloist with many orchestras.

De Sanctis states that his reeds are of approximately the French
type and that they have a fairly short scrape to allow him to get
a robust sonority. The length is that which would be in tune with
the principal Italian orchestras. He uses gold beater's skin on the
reed only when the reed leaks air on the sides. De Sanctis has become accustomed to playing all types of scrape that fit the French
bore oboe.

Date of information: 1959.

Giuseppe Tomassini. Born February 21, 1915, in Ascoli Piceno,
Italy. Tomassini was the First Oboist of the Symphony Orchestra

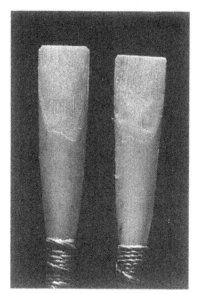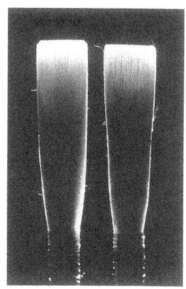

PLATE 37 The reeds of Giuseppe Tomassini

of the National Academy "Santa Cecilia" and teacher of oboe at the "Santa Cecilia" Conservatory of Music in Rome, Italy, until 1977. He studied with Riccardo Scozzi at the same school. Tomassini plays a Lorée oboe with serial number XX 18.

Dates of information: 1958, 1980.

11. NEW ZEALAND

Norman Edwin Booth. Born December 24, 1925, in Timaru, New Zealand. In 1959 Booth was Principal Oboist of the National Orchestra of Wellington, New Zealand. He studied with Horace Green, who at that time was late of the London Philharmonic Orchestra and the BBC Orchestra. Booth also imported instruments to New Zealand; therefore, he was always trying out different ones. The oboe he used at that time was a Howarth, No. 1228, thumb-plate system. He previously played an oboe with the Conservatory system of fingering, but changed because he preferred a different B-flat. Regarding the reeds he uses, Booth makes the following remarks:

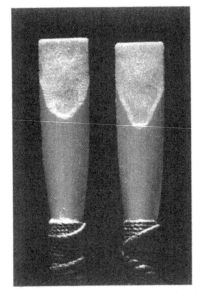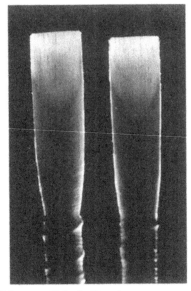

PLATE 38 The reeds of Norman Edwin Booth

I must admit I am one of those people who have one good reed at a time—the one I am using. These reeds [represented in plate 38] are ones I have just made and are not blown in. However, I have scraped them a little more than I usually scrape a new reed to make them blow like one I have blown in. The scrape is fairly representative of how they would look when finished. I use no particular shape of scrape, but vary it for each piece of cane; the more solid the feel of the reed when I press it together, the more I scrape back. I aim at getting a fairly free rattle in the reed when I blow through it with my lips almost to the cork.

I gouge the cane to about .022 of an inch in the center, tapering to .023 of an inch at either end. About 50 percent of the cane so gouged gets as far as being tied on the tube, as all pieces that I can press right flat together with little resistance after they are shaped I do not use.

At the bottom of the scrape, I usually make a decided dip down to the second layer of fibre and taper towards the tip from that point. I use French cane for my oboe reeds, but have some Australian cane for the Cor Anglais which seems as good as the French.

Date of information: 1959.

 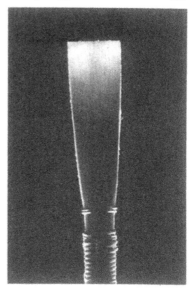

PLATE 39 A reed of Anonymous Leningrad
Symphony player

12. RUSSIA

Leningrad. Anonymous oboist of the Leningrad Symphony around the year 1954.

Anatol Petrov. Born 1913 in Moscow, Russia. In 1959 Petrov was First Oboist of the USSR State Symphony Orchestra, having been associated with this orchestra since 1937. He was also Professor of Oboe at the Tchaikovsky State Conservatory of Music. At the age of fourteen Petrov began to study the oboe with Professor Ivanov of the Moscow Music School. At the age of twenty-one he joined the Bolshoi Theatre Orchestra. He played a German-made Zimmerman oboe, serial number 3182 (1929).

One Petrov reed (not photographed or measured here) was loaned to the writer by David Woolley of Victoria, Australia, who toured Russia as Principal Oboist of the London Philharmonic Orchestra in 1956. Woolley states that many of the oboists in Russia use Zimmerman oboes with an earlier fingering system.

PLATE 40 The reeds of Anatol Petrov

The cane from which that reed was made comes from the Cauca-
sus, which is the region between the Black and Caspian seas, approximately eight hundred miles almost due south of Moscow. The
cane that was given to Woolley by Petrov was wide in diameter,
perhaps 15 millimeters, and had a ribbed bark unlike the smooth
surface favored by oboists of other European countries and
America. It had a rather spongy-looking quality inside, a whitish
green color instead of the usual yellow texture.

The writer later received the reeds in plate 40 from Petrov. It
is these reeds that are measured in Table 3. Woolley's reed was
returned before the extensive measurements were made.

Date of information: 1959.

13. SWITZERLAND

Egon Parolari. Born September 9, 1921, in Brugg/Aargau, Switzerland. In 1957 Parolari was Principal Oboist of the Winterthur
Symphony Orchestra and taught oboe at the Winterthur Conserv-

atory of Music, Winterthur, Switzerland. He has held orchestral positions with the Gstaad Music Festival Week under Hermann Scherchen, the Suisse Romande Orchestra conducted by Ernest Ansermet, the Swiss Festival Orchestra of Luzern since 1944, and others. Parolari has been one of the most sought-after oboe soloists of Europe, appearing in many countries from time to time as soloist with orchestras, chamber orchestras, string quartets, and trios. He toured Spain in 1956 with the Streichtrio Redditi. In 1953 he auditioned and played a concert with the Berlin Philharmonic Orchestra under Wilhelm Furtwängler and was offered the position of First Oboist there, which he did not accept. Parolari won second prize in the International Music Competition in 1952, judged by Scherchen, Ansermet, and Furtwängler. He is a recording artist of considerable distinction and can be heard playing the following works on releases by the Concert Hall Society of New York: (G-6) Concerti for Oboe in D Minor and F Major, Vivaldi; (F-17) Concerto for Two Oboes, Albinoni; (E-17) Concerto de Camera for Flute and English Horn, Honegger; (G-15) Concerto for Violin and Oboe, J. S. Bach; (H-4) *Six Metamorphoses after Ovid for Oboe Alone*, Britten; (CHS-1227) Sinfonie in F Minor for Orchestra and Solo Oboe, Dittersdorf.

From 1936 until 1939 Parolari studied oboe with Marcel Saillet of Zurich. From 1939 until 1943 he attended and was graduated from the Zurich Conservatory. During a stay in Paris (1948–50), he studied with R. Lamorlette. Parolari plays a Marigaux (Paris) oboe, which bears the serial number 1046 and was made in 1942.

Parolari makes the following remarks:

I, myself, have a small collection of oboe reeds, some from American and Australian oboists. The reeds are often very different in relation to the length of the scraped parts and the thickness of the cane. In any case, to me, they all have one thing in common—the avoidance of a [scooped-out place] in the center of the reed. Germans call this wood that is left in the center of the reed "the heart."

The reed, in my opinion, has to be steady, that is to say, large intervals in the upper register must hold [*stehen*] without one having to press or correct with the lips.

These reeds [plate 41] are typical of my making; however, I have

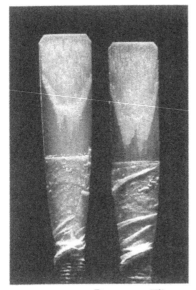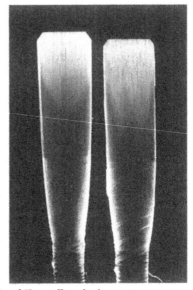

Plate 41 The reeds of Egon Parolari

some feelings about both of them. Number 1 [left-hand reed] is fairly new and is not elastic enough. Number 2 [right-hand reed] is a used reed and is a little too strong.

Date of information: 1957.

14. UNITED STATES

Rhadames J. Angelucci. Born April 1, 1915, in Philadelphia, Pennsylvania. Angelucci joined the Minneapolis Symphony Orchestra in 1936 and played English horn from 1936 until 1938. He became Principal Oboist in 1938 and has remained in that position for the past forty-two years (1938–79). The orchestra is now called the Minnesota Orchestra. Angelucci studied oboe with Louis DiFulvio and attended the Curtis Institute, Philadelphia, Pennsylvania, where he was a student of Marcel Tabuteau's. During the 1950s he played a Lorée oboe, AK 66. Since that time he has played Laubin oboes and other Lorées and is now playing a Gordet.

Angelucci states that the two particular reed examples in plate

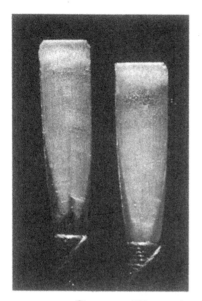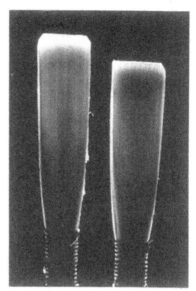

PLATE 42 The reeds of Rhadames Angelucci

42 are not the best, but by looking at them it should be possible for one to get a general idea of some of the opinions he has regarding reedmaking. He states that he scrapes quite a bit from the back and overlaps the blades. His style of reedmaking has remained almost the same over the years.

Dates of information: 1957, 1979.

Leonard Arner. Born September 12, 1923, in New York City. In 1958 Arner was a free-lance player in the New York City area. Some of the positions that he has held include First Oboist with the following orchestras: Buffalo Philharmonic, National Symphony Orchestra (Washington, D.C.), St. Louis Symphony, Symphony of the Air, and the NBC Television Opera. His most recent positions have been oboist with the Chamber Music Society of Lincoln Center and First Oboe of the New York City Opera.

He has studied with Bruno Labate and Rene Corne. In 1957 he played a Laubin oboe with serial number 95.

Dates of information: 1958, 1979.

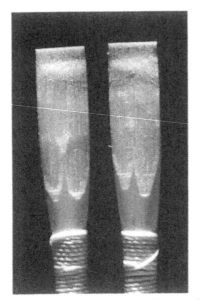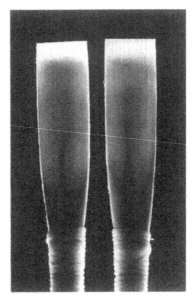

PLATE 43   The reeds of Leonard Arner

Alfred Barthel. Born 1869 (1871?) in Dijon, France. Deceased 1957, Maywood, Illinois. Barthel was Solo Oboe in the Chicago Symphony Orchestra from 1904 until 1928. He then played in the Chicago Civic Opera Orchestra for ten years and was a member of the faculty of the University of Wisconsin at Madison. Before coming to the United States at the invitation of Theodore Thomas, he had played in an orchestra in Algiers and, immediately before coming to the United States, at the Opéra-Comique in Paris. He studied at the Conservatoire with Georges Gillet, winning First Prize in oboe at his graduation in 1891.

The reed in plate 44 has lost its tip over the years. However, the photograph still clearly shows the three areas of the scrape that Barthel recognized. (1) The flat area at the tip is evident and would run uniformly out to the end if it were there. Then, just behind that flat area is (2) a tapered "U"-shaped area up to (3) the "gold" layer just under the rind. Barthel adjusted resistance, etc. by varying those proportions. The total length of his reeds varied from 72 to 73.5 millimeters. The scrape was for only one-third of

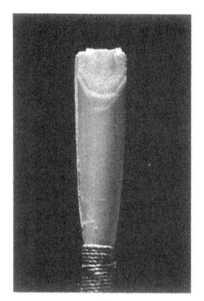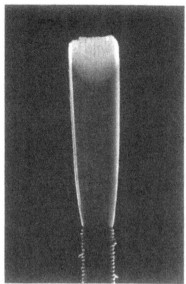

PLATE 44   A reed of Alfred Barthel

the exposed cane length. The cane was gouged .425 millimeters at the center and thinned to not more than .375 millimeters at the edge. Much of the time he used staples made by Frank Kaspar. Major and minor axes of the oval end of Barthel's mandrel are nearly equal (see Table 3). The closer they are to being equal, the higher in pitch the upper octaves will be. In fact, it is said that on a Barthel reed no noticeable change in embouchure is needed to play in the second octave in order to keep it in tune.

Barthel, an outstanding teacher and well-known performer, was almost a legend among oboe players of the Midwest. It is possible that his reed style is a direct link to Georges Gillet.

Date of information: 1957.

Robert Bloom. Born in Pittsburgh, Pennsylvania. His present positions include teaching at the Juilliard School of Music, New York City, and Solo Oboe with the Bach Aria Group (since 1947). He is also Professor Emeritus, Yale University School of Music. Other positions he has held include Assistant First Oboe and English

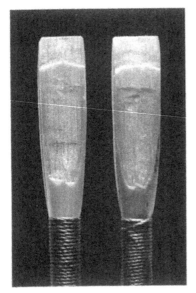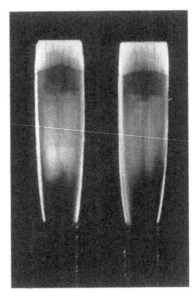

PLATE 45   The reeds of Robert Bloom

Horn of the Philadelphia Orchestra under Stokowski; oboe teacher at the Eastman School of Music, Rochester, New York, and oboist in the Rochester Philharmonic; and Solo Oboe, NBC Symphony Orchestra, under Toscanini. He has been a recording artist for Columbia, RCA, and Capitol records. Bloom studied with Marcel Tabuteau. He plays a Lorée oboe with top joint DS 10 and bottom joint BL 73.

Bloom states that the reeds in plate 45 are rather old and have been played quite a bit, but the general contours correspond to the reeds he generally plays. He remarks, "As you know, one's ideas about reeds do keep changing over the years—these are current examples. My wife, Sara, and I share in the making of reeds."

Date of information: 1980.

Peter Bowman. Born January 10, 1950, in Keene, New Hampshire. Bowman is Principal Oboe of the St. Louis Symphony Orchestra. He is a former First Oboe of the Montreal Symphony and has played on occasion with the Boston Symphony, the Boston Pops,

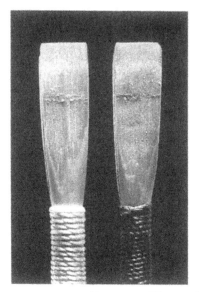 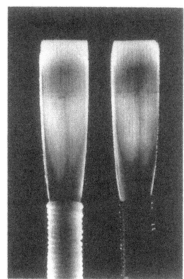

PLATE 46   The reeds of Peter Bowman

the Boston Opera, and the Boston Ballet. He has also been a faculty member at McGill University. Bowman studied with Ralph Gomberg and John Mack and plays Laubin oboe No. 1391.

Bowman makes the following remarks:

> The main thing that I have observed about reedmaking for several years is that what a reed looks like can be terribly insignificant. Since I play a Laubin oboe, generally people have difficulty playing my reeds on Lorées. The biggest secret in reedmaking seems to be hidden in the tip. I have noticed especially in the last 4 years that cane has deteriorated beyond human tolerance, but we try and manage somehow. Because of this, one must be even more critical of his knife ability and try to compensate accordingly.

Date of information: 1980.

Henri de Busscher. Born October 29, 1880, in Brussels, Belgium. Deceased 1978, Los Angeles, California. De Busscher had a long and illustrious career as one of the great oboists of the United States. He supplied the following information: "I was nine years

with Sir Henry Wood in London, as first oboe with the Queen's
Orchestra. For my first six years in the United States, I was first
oboe in the New York Symphony under Walter Damrosch, at the
same time playing in the New York Chamber Music Society.
After this, for a year, my time was entirely taken up by the last
named society. I then came to Los Angeles. . . ." De Busscher
completed twenty-eight years of playing with the Los Angeles
Philharmonic Symphony, playing with the same orchestra during
the summer under various noted conductors in the Hollywood
Bowl. He was also First Oboist for ten years at Columbia Studios
in Hollywood and Oboist for the Ysaye Concerts in Brussels. He
played a Cabart oboe with serial number E 7 and studied with
Guillaume Guidé at the Brussels Conservatoire.

De Busscher made the following remarks: "The two reeds enclosed [plate 47] are representative of the two types I have used.
The French cut (shorter lay) I played up to the time I left New
York. After that, I changed to the Dutch or W cut. The difference, as I analyze it, is that the former demands more embouchure
control to produce roundness of tone. I found the use of the wire
necessary in California because of the lack of humidity, which
closed the reed. The wire helped to control it."

For a short time Gustave Langenus, the clarinetist, published a
magazine entitled the *Woodwind News*. In vol. I, no. 3, of the
year 1926, an article appeared by de Busscher. The following is an
extract from the article that has to do with reeds:

> The oboe is considered one of the most difficult wind instruments
> on account of the very *small* and delicate *double* reed, and while
> speaking of reeds, I would like to mention that I think too many
> oboe players make the mistake of constantly changing their reeds.
> As no two reeds are ever alike, it follows that one must *play* on
> the reed quite a while before knowing just how to humor it. Be-
> sides the great saving of time and nervous energy, the habit of
> using just one fairly good reed is more advantageous than the con-
> tinual changing of reeds in search of a better one.
> I have known many cases where oboe players stayed up all
> night making reeds, the only result being that their work suffered
> in consequence of the nervous strain and their lips were ruined
> by the constant trial of the different reeds. My advice is to use
> as good a reed as possible—and stick to it. I have had many pupils

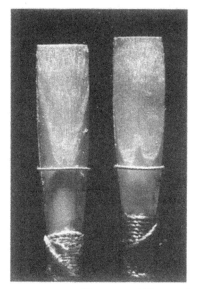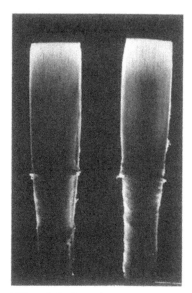

PLATE 47 The reeds of Henri de Busscher

who changed from the study of the flute or clarinet to that of the oboe and all have found the technique of the oboe more difficult than that of their former instruments.

Dates of information: 1957, 1979.

James B. Caldwell. Born December 3, 1938, in Gladewater, Texas. Caldwell is presently Professor of Oboe, Oberlin College Conservatory of Music, Oberlin, Ohio. He joined that institution in 1971. He was oboist with the National Symphony Orchestra, Washington, D.C., 1965–66 and 1968–71, and First Oboe of the Chamber Symphony of Philadelphia, 1966–78. Caldwell studied with Stevens Hewitt and John de Lancie. He plays Lorée oboe BY 40.

Date of information: 1980.

Liliane Lhoest Covington. Born January 5, 1917, in Minneapolis, Minnesota. Covington retired in 1965 as First Oboist at Warner Brothers Studio, Burbank, California. Other positions she has held include First Oboist for RKO, Universal, and Twentieth Century

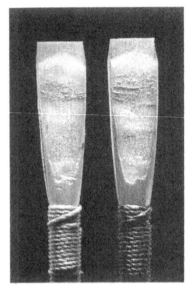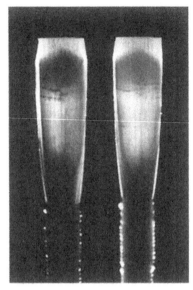

PLATE 48 The reeds of James B. Caldwell

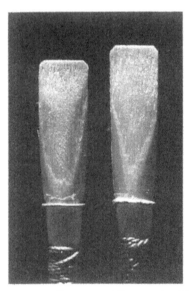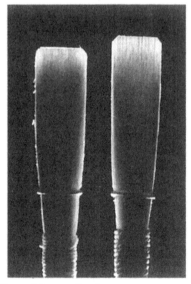

PLATE 49 The reeds of Liliane Lhoest Covington

Fox studios. She studied with Henri de Busscher and Philip Memoli, Jr., and played a Lym oboe with serial number 108.

Covington makes the following remarks: "Cane is so much more responsive on moist or rainy days. Here in California on very dry days, it is hard to get reeds to respond with the proper overtones. I find that oboe reeds for recording should be somewhat thinner than for concert work—as a different style, etc., as a rule, is required."

Dates of information: 1958, 1979.

Marcel J. Dandois. Born December 29, 1890, in Roux, Belgium. Deceased 1970, in Forth Worth, Texas, where he had lived during retirement. During that time he taught oboe at Texas Christian University. Some of the other positions he held include First Oboe, Opéra Théâtre de la Monnaie, Brussels, Belgium; English Horn, Philadelphia Symphony Orchestra; oboe teacher at the College-Conservatory of Music in Cincinnati, Ohio; and, from 1929 until 1956, First Oboist with the Cincinnati Symphony Orchestra. He studied oboe with Professor Guillaume Guidé and Monsieur Piérard, Assistant Professor at the Brussels Conservatory of Music. He played a Lorée oboe with serial number RR 9.

About the reeds in plate 50, Dandois stated:

Reed 1 [far left] is about the same as I played for most of my career. It is about the same as my teacher, Guidé, was playing. It is made of Var cane gouged .025 of an inch. Reed 2 [second from left] is what I am playing now since June 1957. This is the result of experiments I made years ago and have had time to improve since coming here. The lay is short because part of the work is done inside. The gouging is .022–.027 of an inch, same cane and same shaper as Reed 1. I think Reed 2 is superior to Reed 1 in tone quality and intonation. The basis of my last experiment is not new. The French [have been using it for many years]—[with] more or less tapering. My earlier mistake was to make a lay that was too long. I also have altered the thickness of the tapering and its position (one third of the cane). I could not say exactly how much in millimeters.

To make reedmaking easier for my pupils, I teach that subject by measurements. Length of reed, 72 to 74 mm., according to the thickness of the cane and the pitch of the instrument; width, 7 1/3

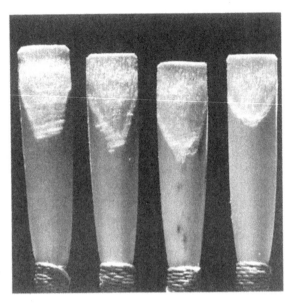

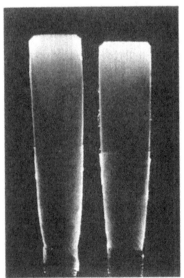 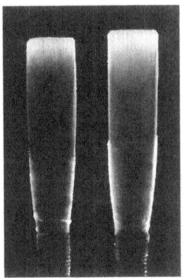

PLATE 50　The reeds of Marcel Dandois

mm.; length of lay, 12 to 13 mm. in [a] V [scrape], always counting the knife strokes—20 each side on 6 mm. of the top and pro-
ceeding down to 12 mm. by equal number of strokes. Test: without the instrument, [play] the notes about do, si, la, sol, fa♯. With
little change except in my last experiment, I have followed the
directions of my teacher.

If everyone [i.e., all oboists] had the same conception of tone,
it would be simple to standardize reedmaking. However, each
seems to have a different opinion of tone quality. I found that
the French type of reed gives flexibility and a penetrating tone
with the minimum of blowing. The ones I am using now still are
easier on the lips and produce a better quality of tone and intonation, especially for the octaves. With the new style, it is possible
to keep the maximum of bark on the cane; that helps to increase
the pastoral color of the oboe tone and prevent early closing of
the reed. To have a dark tone, the cane has to be thick and,
consequently, hard blowing, or the bark nearly scraped off and,
therefore, the intonation becomes insecure. One likes the tone
which he is accustomed to hearing, and it is good if it (the oboe)
does not lose its characteristic quality by sounding like another
instrument, such as the clarinet or flute. It must be bright and
penetrating, though easy to play.

There is an article about Marcel Dandois by Francis Estes in *To
the World's Oboists*, vol. I, no. 3, December 1973.

Dates of information: 1958, 1979.

Alexandre Duvoir. Born 1889 in Paris, France. Deceased 1979,
Los Angeles, California. Some of the more notable positions that
he held are First Oboist of the Minneapolis Symphony for eighteen years, First Oboist of RKO Studios for ten years, and First
Oboist of the Los Angeles Chamber Symphony. For a number of
years before his retirement he was Professor of Oboe at the University of Southern California. Duvoir began his study of the oboe
with Fernand Gillet and then studied with Georges Gillet at the
Paris Conservatory. He played a Lorée oboe with serial number
LL 4.

Duvoir made the following remarks:

> . . . As you know, reeds are made according to the current occu-
> pation, and also, another very important point is the place where
> you are living. For instance, in my own experience, I played dif-

ferent reeds in France, where the climate is damp and mild, than when I came to this country to Minneapolis, where the climate is dry and cold. Then we had a winter tour, leaving Minneapolis in January for four to six weeks, going south to New Orleans, Miami, etc., traveling in weather from below zero, dry, to 70 plus, humid. In order to be able to maintain my standard of playing, I had to make my reeds as I was traveling; the best Minneapolis reeds could not play well in New Orleans! Now, when I came to California, which is warm and dry, I encountered those treacherous microphones in the moving picture studios. Thus, I had to play with an easier reed and develop a smaller tone.

The two reeds [plate 51] are the type I am playing now and are very much the same as I used in France. They are made on new Lorée tubes, have never been played, so might change a little, probably will close, and are very good for me. I chose them from among two dozen that I made recently. . . . May I suggest that you collect some samples of *second oboe players,* as you know they have sometimes a more difficult range in which to play and so should make reeds accordingly.

Dates of information: 1958, 1979.

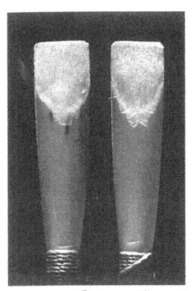

PLATE 51   The reeds of Alexandre Duvoir

Bert Gassman. Born 1911. In 1958 Gassman was First Oboist of the Los Angeles Philharmonic Orchestra. Some of the other positions he has held include First Oboe and English Horn of the Cleveland Symphony Orchestra and First Oboe and English Horn of the Metropolitan Opera Orchestra. Gassman has studied with Pierre Mathieu, Marcel Tabuteau, and Dirk van Emmerik. He plays a Laubin oboe, serial number 109, and Lorée AK 31.

Gassman makes the following interesting remarks about his change of reed style: "During the first period of my career of 30 years, the instruction and playing style was the clear, brilliant, typical French oboe sound obtained with a thin gouged cane, short scrape U, and very thin tip. Tabuteau, who later instructed me, stated that he himself wished for a darker tone; so I changed the scrape, as you see, to the long scrape, almost to the silk, to darken the sound. Again the trend seems to be back to the clear French tone."

Date of information: 1958.

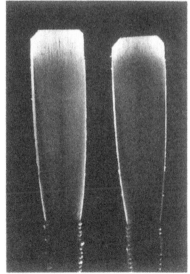

PLATE 52 The reeds of Bert Gassman

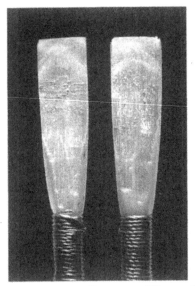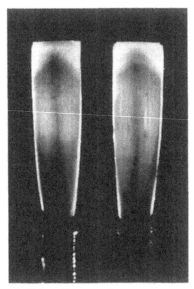

PLATE 53 The reeds of Elden Gatwood

Elden Gatwood. Born December 12, 1926, in Nashville, Tennessee.
Gatwood is First Oboe of the Pittsburgh Symphony Orchestra.
He has also held positions as Second Oboe in the Cleveland Sym-
phony Orchestra and Second Oboe and English Horn in the Casals
Festival Orchestras. He studied with Bruno Labate, Lois Wann,
Philip Kirchner, and Robert Bloom. He plays Lorée oboe CJ 33.

Gatwood makes the following remarks: "It has been touch and
go since I started. Not one teacher I studied with showed me one
thing about reedmaking, so it has been 26 years in orchestras plus
the time in school that I have struggled trying to come up with
workable reeds. I think when one learns through trial and error
there tends to be more insecurity and resultant excessive experimentation."

Date of information: 1979.

Fernand Gillet. Born October 15, 1882, in Paris, France. At this
time (1979) Mr. Gillet is retired from a long and illustrious career
of seventy-four years of playing and teaching. Positions he has

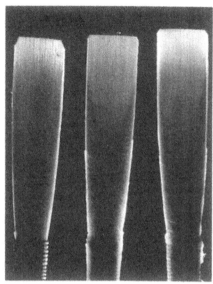

PLATE 54 The reeds of Fernand Gillet

held include First Oboe of the Paris Opéra, twenty-four years; First Oboe, Boston Symphony Orchestra, 1925–46, during which time he taught at the New England Conservatory. He also served as a faculty member of Boston University, and he taught master classes at Montreal Conservatory from 1946 until 1952. Gillet received the honorary Doctor of Music degree from the New England Conservatory and the Eastman School of Music.

Gillet was a student of Georges Gillet, his uncle, at the Paris Conservatory. He was graduated from that institution with First Prize in 1898. He plays Lorée oboe CC 85.

Gillet makes the following remarks:

> These three reeds [plate 54] are according to the pattern I used to play and are made by de Vergie, Second Oboist of the Boston Symphony. De Vergie used to fix all of my reeds when I was in activity. . . . I never made my reeds—no patience; in this line I do not pretend to be right. Earlier in my career I played on reeds made by Arthur Bridet.
>
> You will notice that, according to the present oboe players in

America, these reeds will be called old-fashioned. They are, however, confusing *a ringing tone* with a reedy tone, for they like to have a tone something between a saxophone and a clarinet. It is just as if you put a muffler on a beautiful Stradivarius violin.

Gillet goes on to add that the exponents of the darker sound may think that the sound of the Stradivarius is old-fashioned also, and perhaps would prefer a "Sears-Roebuck" one better! He states, "In my opinion, the oboe should match the violin, the English horn match the viola, and the bassoon match the 'cello." Commenting on his uncle's reeds, Gillet states, ". . . he gouged his cane himself and before folding the cane he let it dry *three years*. Today, to avoid that lapse of time, they cook the cane, as you may know, and, of course, it is not so natural."

There is an excellent article about Fernand Gillet by Jean Northrup, a former Gillet student, in *To the World's Oboists,* vol. V, September 1977.

Dates of information: 1958, 1979.

Harold Gomberg. Born November 30, 1918, in Malden, Massachusetts. Gomberg joined the New York Philharmonic Orchestra as Solo Oboist at the beginning of the 1943–44 season. He retired from that position at the end of the 1976–77 season. He has also been Solo Oboist in the Toronto Symphony and the St. Louis Symphony. In 1957 Gomberg was playing a Laubin experimental model oboe. He studied with Marcel Tabuteau.

Gomberg states that the reed pictured in plate 55 is generally representative of the type of reed he uses. However, he has used many oboes in past years, and his type of reed differs somewhat with the changing timbre of each instrument.

Dates of information: 1957, 1979.

Ralph Gomberg. Born June 18, 1921, in Boston, Massachusetts. At present (1979) Ralph Gomberg is First Oboist of the Boston Symphony Orchestra and is an Adjunct Professor (Oboe) at Boston University. For many years he played a Gomberg Brothers oboe and presently plays a Laubin 1400 series.

Gomberg states:

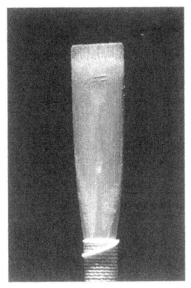

PLATE 55 A reed of Harold Gomberg

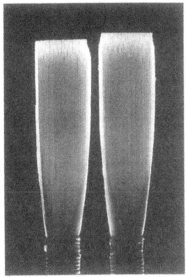

PLATE 56 The reeds of Ralph Gomberg

The individual oboist must have a clear idea of what sound he wants to produce before he can make a good reed for himself. This is the crux of the matter. In all my years of traveling over the world talking and listening to other oboists I have discovered the one incontrovertible fact—that they play the way they want to play because of the acoustical demands of their own ears. I have exchanged reeds with many oboists and their sounds do not change that radically when they play with my reed, and somehow I can get more of my sound from their reed. Coincidentally, this ties in very much with statements made by violinists when they speak of the different [individually typical] sounds they get on the *same* violin passed from one to another.

Dates of information: 1958, 1979.

Earnest Harrison. Born July 13, 1918, in Moberly, Missouri. Harrison joined the faculty of the Louisiana State University in 1966 and is presently Professor of Oboe at that institution. He has also taught at the University of Kentucky, American University, and George Washington University. He has held orchestral positions in the Rochester Philharmonic Orchestra, Houston Symphony, and the San Antonio Symphony. Immediately prior to his present position he was First Oboist of the National Symphony Orchestra, Washington, D.C. He has studied with Rene Corne, Alfred Hicks, Robert Sprenkle, and John Minsker. He has played a Chauvet oboe with serial number B.W. 160 and is presently playing a Lorée oboe CT 69.

Harrison makes the following remarks:

I use a variety of shapes [Tabuteau, Minsker, Brannen, Angelo, Prestini]. The size of my reeds varies between 68 mm. and 71–72 mm. depending on the width of the shape and the basic dimension of the tube cane which affects the size of the opening. I use both silver and brass tubes mostly 47 mm. in length. The average overall length is 70 mm. However, specifications are only numbers and the dimensions of a given reed are relative to all the factors present—overall length of reed, width of the shape and the amount of opening at the tip. I try to be consistent in building the reed to pitch (crow a solid sound as opposed to a rattle) an octave sound with the lower partial predominant. The crow of a C is my aim; however, reeds that crow sharper or flatter also

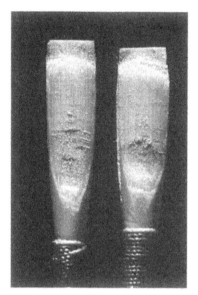 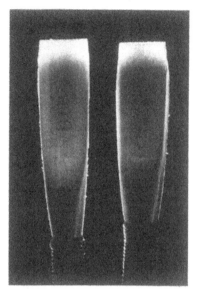

PLATE 57 The reeds of Earnest Harrison

work if you can be flexible enough to adjust your embouchure
to the reed. I try to play with a reed that is built up to pitch
with my mouth open as opposed to biting the pitch up. My tips
now average from 2.5 to 4 mm. I do not take the cane off all the
way to the thread, but leave some cane (approximately 5 mm.)
from the top end of the tube to the bottom of the scrape.

Dates of information: 1958, 1979.

Philip Kirchner. Born March 11, 1890, in Wilna, Russia. Deceased
1970, Cleveland, Ohio. Kirchner's playing positions included the
Symphony of the Air, NBC Opera, and the City Center Ballet. He
was also associated with the New York Philharmonic Symphony,
Sousa's Band, the Barrere Ensemble, the Cleveland Symphony, the
NBC Symphony, and many other musical organizations. Kirchner
studied with Bruno Labate and was the first U.S. student of Marcel
Tabuteau. He played a Lorée oboe with serial number AJ 98.

Kirchner remarked: "In my opinion, most oboists in the United
States owe Tabuteau a debt of gratitude. He established our pres-

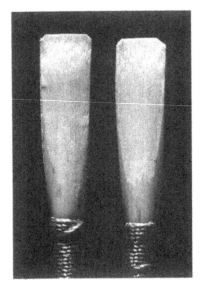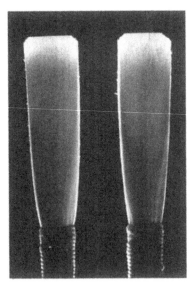

PLATE 58 The reeds of Philip Kirchner

ent school of oboe playing. Heretofore, there had been none. Regarding reeds, with some variation, all of Tabuteau's students use the same system of reedmaking—the long scrape."

Dates of information: 1958, 1980.

Arthur Krilov. Born August 22, 1922, in New York City. In 1958 Krilov was the First Oboist of the Pittsburgh Symphony Orchestra. Prior to that position, he was First Oboist of the Dallas Symphony Orchestra. He plays a Lorée oboe with serial number AS 61.

Krilov remarks:

I studied with Maxim Waldo of New York City when in high school, but after that with no one. My playing is a result of my own work over the years, and while my reeds may bear some resemblance to others, they fall within no particular school, so far as I know. The two reeds I include are ones that I have used this season. They are too old now to be of use for playing, but they were quite good in their youth. I think they will show some

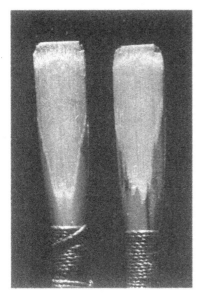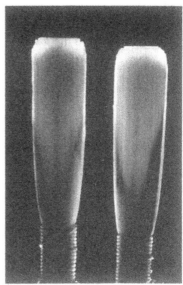

PLATE 59 The reeds of Arthur Krilov

things you may find of value since neither is a freak, as so many good ones turn out. They are somewhat weaker to me since they are from the early part of the season. The word "weaker" is, of course, a word I use to describe a reaction. Your set of words may be different . . . it would seem that much of the important things that make reeds "good" are too intangible to be written down.

Date of information: 1958.

Marc Lifschey. Born June 16, 1926, in New York City. In 1958 Lifschey was the First Oboist of the Cleveland Symphony Orchestra. He has also played First Oboe in the Buffalo Philharmonic, First Oboe in the National Symphony Orchestra, and First Oboe in the Metropolitan Opera Orchestra. Lifschey has studied with Fernand Gillet, Bert Brenner, and Marcel Tabuteau. He plays Lorée oboe AY 42.

Date of information: 1958.

John Mack. Born October 30, 1927, in Somerville, New Jersey.

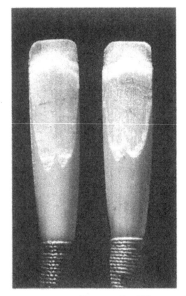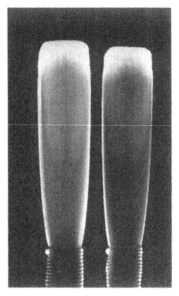

Plate 60 The reeds of Marc Lifschey

He is Solo Oboe of the Cleveland Symphony Orchestra, a position he has held since 1965. He was Solo Oboe of the New Orleans Symphony, 1952–63, and the National Symphony Orchestra, Washington, D.C., 1963–65. Other positions he has held include First Oboe, Sadler's Wells Ballet Orchestra; Assistant Oboe to Marcel Tabuteau in three Casals Festivals; First Oboe, Brevard Music Festival; First Oboe, Bethlehem Bach Festival; First Oboe, New Orleans Opera. Mack has studied with Labate, Storch, Minsker, H. Gomberg, and Tabuteau. In 1958 he played Lorée oboes AX 63 and AV 36.

In 1958 Mack stated that reeds 1 and 2 (reeds numbered from left to right, plate 61) had been used in concerts, the larger one on the AX oboe, the other on the AV. He rated the staples as excellent.

Reeds 3 and 4 are from 1979 and are made for Lorée oboes DS 84, EW 41, and ES 01. Mack uses a Pfeifer shaper tip (Mack curve #1) and 46.5-millimeter Lorée tubes. He gouges cane approximately .58–.45 millimeters.

Dates of information: 1958, 1979.

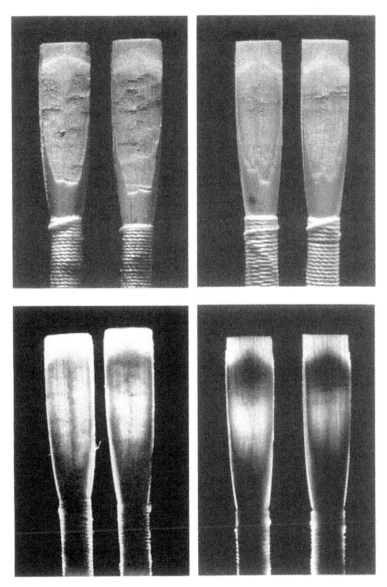

PLATE 61 The reeds of John Mack

Arno Mariotti. Born October 6, 1911. Mariotti has been Professor of Oboe at the University of Michigan, Ann Arbor, since about 1973. Prior to that time he was Principal Oboist of the Detroit Symphony Orchestra. Other positions he has held include First Oboe of the Indianapolis Symphony for seven years and First Oboe of the Pittsburgh Symphony for eight years. He played four summers as First Oboe with the Robin Hood Dell Orchestra in Philadelphia, and for at least eleven years was First Oboe with the Chautauqua Symphony at Chautauqua, New York. Mariotti was graduated from the Curtis Institute, where he was a student of Marcel Tabuteau's. In 1958 he played Lorée oboes AK 91 and AU 31.

Date of information: 1958.

Philip Memoli. Born August 13, 1900, in Birmingham, Alabama. Memoli retired from the Metro-Goldwyn-Mayer Studio Orchestra in 1956 after being with them for twenty-three years. Some of the other organizations with which he has been associated include

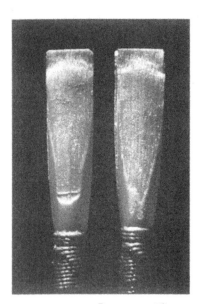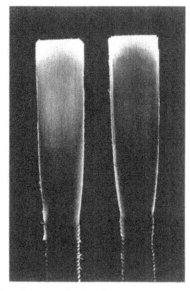

PLATE 62   The reeds of Arno Mariotti

the Los Angeles Philharmonic Orchestra for thirteen years and the Hollywood Bowl Orchestra. Memoli studied with Albert de Busscher and Henri de Busscher. He plays a Cabart oboe.

Memoli remarks:

> It is gratifying to see that your approach to this complex problem of reeds is based on such sound basic logic. I agree completely that the reed one uses *has* to coincide with not only the position one holds, that is, type of ensemble and situation, but definitely upon his idea also of how an oboe should sound. I have held firmly to the belief that the oboe is essentially a vibrant sound; not nasal, mind you, but definitely not the dark sound that some of my colleagues have championed. My idea is still the old school of a delicate sound accompanied by a broad range of coloring, which lends more to shading and artistry. This can of course be done with the so-called dark sound, but naturally on a narrower basis. . . . I definitely consider Henri de Busscher one of the greatest oboists. . . .

Dates of information: 1957, 1980.

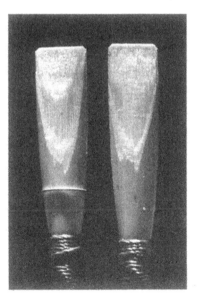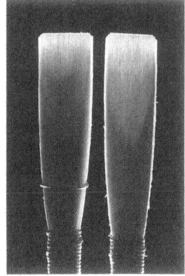

PLATE 63 The reeds of Philip Memoli

Florian F. Mueller. Born June 15, 1904. Mueller retired in 1973 as Professor of Oboe and Wind Instruments Literature at the University of Michigan, Ann Arbor. He joined the Chicago Symphony Orchestra in 1927 and became Solo Oboist in 1931, a position he held until his retirement from the orchestra in 1954. Some of the other positions he has held include First Oboe of Sousa's Band, First Oboe of the Rochester Philharmonic, and Associate Professor of Theory and Chairman of the Department of Wind Instruments, Roosevelt University, Chicago, Illinois. Mueller studied oboe with Alfred Barthel. He plays Lorée oboe AC 32 and Lucerne oboes 468 and 435.

In 1958 Mueller made the following remarks:

These two reeds [plate 64] are made with the measurements I am now using, but I have changed my reedmaking style several times in my career. However, this one is the most satisfactory to me and to my pupils. I have found the Lorée oboe consistently flat— I have owned about seven at one time or another; hence, the shortened tube to give me a little leeway with tuning.

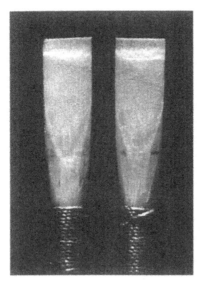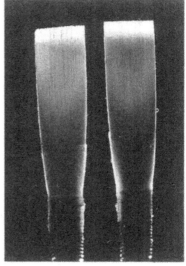

PLATE 64 The reeds of Florian Mueller

My teacher, Mr. Barthel, brought me up on a very short scrape reed. His cane measured .45 mm. at both center and sides—and consequently the facing was very short. My shaper is supposed to be a copy of the one used by Gillet, Sr.

In 1979 Mueller stated that the only change in his reed style from the photographed examples was that the facing of his present reeds had been lengthened about 3 millimeters and that there was a more pronounced spine toward the tip of the reed.

Dates of information: 1958, 1979.

Loyd Rathbun. Born June 2, 1911, in Los Angeles, California. Rathbun retired from professional playing in 1959, when he left Warner Brothers Motion Picture Studios, Hollywood, California. From 1962 until the end of 1974 he was Library Head at the M.I.T. Lincoln Laboratory. Other positions he has held include First Oboe of the Kansas City Philharmonic Orchestra and oboist in Werner Jannsen's Hollywood Symphony Orchestra and the Ojai Festival Orchestra. He has made free-lance studio recordings and served as oboist with several community symphonies. Rathbun taught for ten years at the University of Southern California. He studied with Philip Memoli, Jr., and Henri de Busscher. He plays a Cabart oboe with serial number Y 40. His other instruments are the Cabart oboe d'amore number I 138, Cabart English horn number X 87, and Lorée baritone oboe number O 60. Regarding the other instruments that he plays, Rathbun says, "For their bigger pictures, the composers of motion picture background scores are always looking for new or different tone colors, and I use both of the uncommon instruments frequently. *Rebel without a Cause* was the latest picture using the baritone oboe, though an old picture recently released on TV, *Objective Burma*, has the longest and most obvious solos in it."

Rathbun makes the following remarks about the reeds he supplied for plate 66:

I played both of these reeds in a concert this afternoon. *For my embouchure* they are excellent—almost sorry to send them away. But I got four good reeds from five pieces of cane when I made these. The fifth one split before it was playable at all.

I think that this style of scraping requires playing with the embouchure for which it was made more than many types of scraping. Because they probably will not sound nor respond well for you, I want to repeat that they are top quality for me. I wish to add a word of explanation concerning the wire collars you will find on them. These are frowned upon by many players, particularly in or from the East. I can only feel sorry for them. My percentage of good reeds is far higher than that of most players, and I worry the least of any I know. It is no less logical to put a collar on an oboe reed than it is to put one on an English horn or oboe d'amore reed. The collar permits a ready correction of the opening, the reed can be made to blow easier without sacrifice of tone, and the wire can overcome inaccurate shaping or faults of binding onto the tube.

A wire collar put on a reed which is already playing will deaden the sound and cause it to play "harder," but this is corrected by more scraping just as when the same condition exists before or without a wire. A reed can be made to produce the same tone quality either with or without the collar.

Rathbun uses a dial indicator gage (plate 65) as an aid in his reedmaking. The following is his explanation of his dial indicator and also his technique of using it:

PLATE 65 Dial indicator

For the serious student and professional oboist, a useful instrument has been developed recently—a stock model dial indicator gage so mounted that it can be used to measure the thickness in thousandths of an inch at any given spot on either blade of an oboe or bassoon reed. With this gage, it is possible to scrape a reed to perfect symmetry. Each blade of the reed can be tapered identically, from the center of the tip to the back of the lay, and the four sides of the lay (opposite points on each blade) can be made equal at any given point. Considering that it is correct balance which makes an excellent reed from a good piece of cane, it is easy to see how valuable this instrument can be. The bassoon players Don Christlieb, who first devised it, and Ray Nowlin, who has done considerable experimenting with it, have even arrived at a standard of thickness and proportion, and now make their reeds to specification. Reeds finished according to this predetermined standard require far less touching up than usually given any new reed as it is "played in." So far no oboist has developed such a standard, for in the smaller oboe reed, differences in thickness too slight to record on a practical measuring instrument change the playing of a reed considerably. The gage is used to bring the oboe reed to a state of relative proportion within a thousandth of an inch, and then further scraping is done on those areas which the oboist knows will bring the response he desired, the balance being maintained by accurately counting the touching-up knife strokes.

The gage in the illustration is made by the Federal Products Corporation, 1144 Eddy Street, Providence, Rhode Island. It is equally adaptable to oboe or bassoon reedmaking. It is Model V81, Full Jeweled, 0-100 Direct Reading Dial, with a 7/16-inch Taper Point. . . . The clamps which hold the horizontal rods to the upright are Brown and Sharpe Swivel Clamps for 740 Test Set . . . and may be purchased from the dealer who sells the gage. There is additional expense for the heavy base with the upright rod, the rod to hold the gage, and the rod with the needle-like end which slips between the ends of the reed, all of which will have to be made or obtained from a machinist. The "needle" end for oboe reeds is about 1/16 of an inch wide and 3/4 of an inch long. It is flattened slightly to the shape of an oval or ellipse, as viewed from the end, to fit more easily between the blades of the reed when measuring the sides of the lay, and it tapers in thickness from slightly over 1/32 of an inch at the base to less than 1/32 of an inch at the tip. However, the upper side at the very tip has a minute hump in order to give a raised striking spot to the gage point. The scorings on the needle are arbitrarily spaced 2 mm. apart, beginning at the tip. A needle proportionately longer and heavier is used for bassoon reeds.

The same model of the above gage supplied with "Plain" bearings instead of the "Full Jeweled" is considerably cheaper, but it is not recommended. The "Full Jeweled" one is advised for the utmost smoothness of action that is necessary in this process in which there are still too many variables. The gage measuring in the thousandths of an inch is best, it is also felt. One constructed to measure divisions smaller than one thousandth is too sensitive for measuring cane against a comparatively flexible needle; readings will be inconsistent and confusing. Even if successful, such accuracy would be of no practical value.

The author's technique of using this instrument is as follows: The reed is scraped in the usual way until it is almost thin enough. Then one blade of the reed is given an identification mark, as blade 1. Of course, blade 2, the other blade, needs no mark. First, measurements are taken in a line down the center of each blade. The reed is put on the needle to the place where the gage will measure the thickness at a spot on blade 1 at the very heel of the lay. This measurement is written down to be followed in a vertical column by the measurements at each succeeding point toward the tip. The measurements for blade 2 will be put down in another column several spaces to the right of column 1. Now the measurements are compared and circles put around the figures which are larger than those in the corresponding positions on the other blade. Additional scraping is then given to the indicated spots. When the centers are satisfactorily equal, the sides of the lay are measured. It is best to record these thickness figures in a logical relation to the others, i.e., the measurements for the right side of the lay of blade 1 at the right side of column 1, etc. When the four lines of measurements are taken (right and left side of each blade), then these thicknesses are equalized. If the reed is now nearly ready to play, it can be finished to the desired tone quality and response by the usual touching-up methods, but the perfect balance is always kept by counting the touching-up strokes.

The reed, placed on the needle, should be measured with only the spring tension of the gage point holding it in place. If possible, the dealer or a service man should tighten the tension of this spring considerably for reed measuring. However, if, in putting it on the needle, the reed is tilted slightly down at the cork, making the tip press up on the gage point, it may cause the indicator to record differently than if it had been pointed upward. A little experimentation is necessary to determine how to place the reed on the needle to get consistent readings.

Let me say that I never make a reed anymore without using the gage. It takes just as long as without, but chances are much more than doubled that the reed will be good. It is especially helpful with an English horn reed, the thickness of which is not as easy to judge by eye. Other oboists and bassoonists here in Los Angeles who have gages feel the same way about them. We would have them even if the cost was much greater.

Table 2 shows Rathbun's gage reading for his two reeds. Rathbun states, "Of course, even after corrections to balance the scrapings, I took more cane off to make them play properly. These readings mean nothing as to the thickness of the finished reeds."

TABLE 2

Dial Indicator Measurements for
Loyd Rathbun's Reeds

REED 1

	Blade 1			Blade 2	
Left	+	Right	Left	+	Right
	23			⌈25⌉ 24	
(21)	20	20	20	23 | 20	(22)
(20)	10	18	19	21 | 19	19
(18)	17	16	17	19 | (18)	(18)
14	6	14	14	18 | 16	(15)
9	12	(11)	(11)	15 | (14)	(12)
6	8	6	5	⌊11⌋ (10)	(7)

REED 2

	22			22	
19	20	(20)	(21)	20	(20)
16	17	(18)	(18)	17	17
13	14	(16)	(16)	14	14
8	12	(12)	11	12	11
4	5	(9)	5	8	(7)

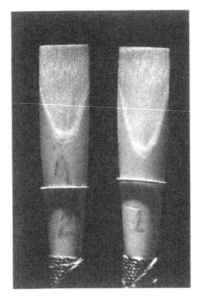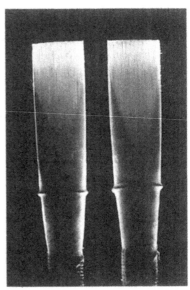

PLATE 66 The reeds of Loyd Rathbun

In 1979 Rathbun continued to play Cabart oboe Y 40. He also continued to make reeds with the help of a dial indicator gage, which met his professional requirements in a high percentage of cases—66 percent to 75 percent.

Dates of information: 1958, 1979.

Merrill Remington (1904–66) was First Oboist of the San Francisco Symphony from 1938 until his retirement in 1964. He was also First Oboist of the San Francisco Opera from 1936 until about 1958. He had also held positions with the NBC Staff Orchestra from 1929 to 1934, the Portland Symphony from 1934 to 1937, and the Hollywood Bowl Orchestra from 1940 to 1946. Remington studied with Alexandre Duvoir and Henri de Busscher. He played a Marigaux oboe with serial number 2417.

Remington stated that no two of his reeds ever looked alike; consequently, he doubts if any definite pattern can be drawn from them.

Dates of information: 1958, 1979.

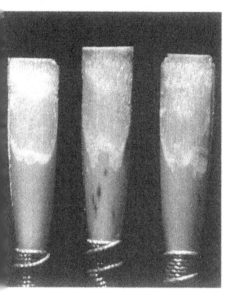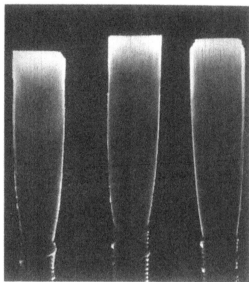

PLATE 67 The reeds of Merrill Remington

Paolo Renzi. Born August 22, 1894, in Rome, Italy. Deceased 1963, New York City. Renzi was First Oboist of the Symphony of the Air (formerly the NBC Symphony). His other positions included First Oboist with the Royal Opera House Orchestra in Rome, Italy; Sousa's Band; the Metropolitan Opera Company for three seasons; the Chicago Civic Opera Company for nine seasons; and the NBC Symphony Orchestra under Arturo Toscanini from 1943 until 1954. He was an oboe student of Riccardo Scozzi's at the Santa Cecilia Conservatory in Rome, Italy, and was graduated from the school in 1914. At the conservatory he also studied piano, composition, and conducting under Bernardino Molinari, and studied under his father, Remigio Renzi, who taught organ and composition. His father was also Principal Organist of the Vatican. Renzi's son, Paul, Jr., is now First Flutist of the San Francisco Symphony and was formerly with Renzi in the NBC as First Flutist.

Dates of information: 1958, 1979.

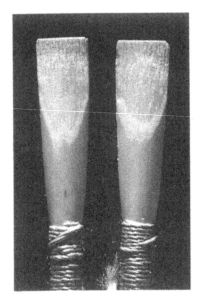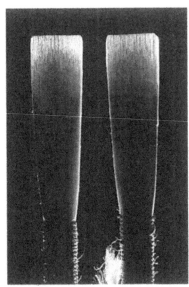

Plate 68 The reeds of Paolo Renzi

Joseph Rizzo (1920–). In 1958 Rizzo was a free-lance oboist in the Los Angeles area. He played at Disney Studios and was First Oboist at the Greek Theater. Other positions he held include oboist in the NBC Symphony and First Oboist of the Houston Symphony, the Kansas City Philharmonic, and the Los Angeles Philharmonic Orchestras. He studied with Clement Lenom and Fernand Gillet. Rizzo played a Lorée oboe with serial number AH 2.

Rizzo is of the opinion that, rather than limit their sound production, pupils should develop an embouchure so that reeds can be *made* to play. Reeds should not be weak. He states that in recording one faces the opposite situation from live performance— that is, volume is secondary to quality, and quality and smoothness are paramount. Regarding his reeds shown in plate 69, he remarks, "These two reeds are interesting because the longer one is the one I used when I studied in Paris in 1947. The shorter one is the reed I used in the motion picture 'Around the World in 80 Days.' Notice the evolution to a shorter, wider reed to give a fuller, less nasal sound."

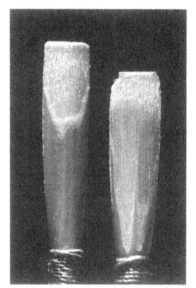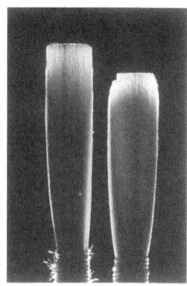

PLATE 69 The reeds of Joseph Rizzo

Date of information: 1958.

Joseph Robinson. Born June 20, 1940, in Lenoir, North Carolina. Robinson is Solo Oboe of the New York Philharmonic Orchestra. Other positions that he has held include Principal Oboe, Atlanta Symphony Orchestra; Assistant Professor of Music at the University of Maryland; and Instructor of Oboe and Chamber Music at the North Carolina School of the Arts. He studied with Marcel Tabuteau and John Mack. Robinson plays Lorée oboes EO 50 and DI 16.

Robinson makes the following remarks: "If there is an overriding principle which has guided the evolution of American reeds, as opposed to typical European ones, it is that the reed should have built into itself the structural elements necessary to provide ease of response, richness of tone, and stability of pitch without resort to the external supports and constraints of embouchure to achieve these attributes."

Date of information: 1979.

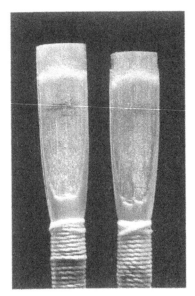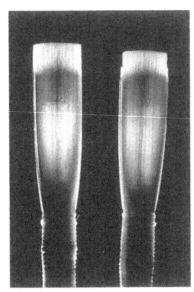

Plate 70 The reeds of Joseph Robinson

Ronald Roseman. Born March 15, 1933, in Brooklyn, New York. He has held positions as acting coprincipal oboe in the New York Philharmonic during the years 1973–74 and 1977–78; Oboist, New York Pro Musica, in the years 1957 through 1970; and Oboist in the Casals Festival Orchestras. His present positions include Oboist, New York Woodwind Quintet; Principal Oboist, "Y" Chamber Orchestra; Member, New York Philomusica; Associate Professor (Adjunct), Yale University School of Music; Faculty, Juilliard School of Music; Artist-in-Residence, State University of New York at Stony Brook. He studied with Lois Wann and Harold Gomberg. He plays Lorée oboe CU 89.

Roseman makes the following remarks:

The red reed [the left-hand reed in both photographs, plate 71] is a bit more typical in that I usually displace reeds to the right.

The dot of bark in the middle of the reed is the result of leaving a little bit of the center spine. I start my reeds by shaping a long, rather thick tip with a triangular shape. I put the back of the tip [see the circle in the accompanying sketch] at about 18.5 mm

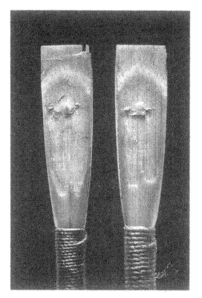 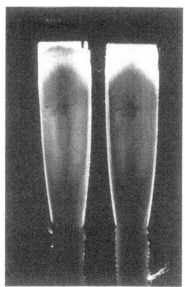

PLATE 71 The reeds of Ronald Roseman

from the string. I scrape the heart and the back leaving a bark spine and bark on the sides (up to the back of the tip). The top of the spine is 16 mm [from the string]. I then put the reed away, and don't take the bark off the back line until the second day. The "dot" is the top of this line. I make my reeds very slowly, taking about 5–6 days to finish them. However, they then last a long time. I gradually thin and shorten the tip and scrape the back during the next few days. I take little wood off the heart after the second day.

I measure the dimensions of the reed quite carefully. The gouge is 60–45.

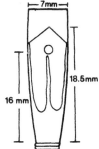

Date of information: 1979.

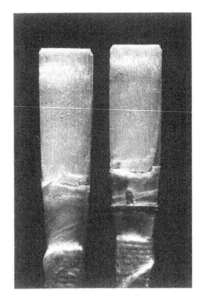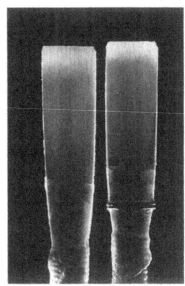

PLATE 72 The reeds of Myron Russell

Myron E. Russell. Born October 18, 1904, in Stafford, Kansas. Russell is presently retired from his position at the University of Northern Iowa. He served that institution for forty-four years (1929–73) as faculty member and music department head (1951–72). He has played with the St. Louis Symphony Orchestra and Bachman's Million Dollar Band. He is well known as a player and conductor. Russell studied with Harold Wheeler, Alfred Barthel, and Robert Forman. He plays Lorée oboe No. ZZ 85.

Dates of information: 1958, 1979.

Gordon Schoneberg. Born December 8, 1919, in Chicago, Illinois. At present Schoneberg is affiliated with California State University–Long Beach as a teacher. He is also a free-lance player and teacher in the Los Angeles area. In 1958 he was First Oboist at Walt Disney Studios in Hollywood. Other positions he has held include First Oboe of the Kansas City Philharmonic; Second Oboe of the Hollywood Bowl Orchestra; Oboist for NBC Red Network Staff Orchestra in Los Angeles, Lux Theatre, and Paul Whiteman Hall of Fame; First Oboe of the Society of Independent Producers Orchestra; and many others. His main teachers were Arnold Kraushaar, Philip Memoli, Jr., and Henri de Busscher. Earlier in his career he used a Lym oboe with serial number 89, but played for some time on Lym number 19.

Schoneberg made the following remarks about his reeds in 1958:

> I do not play the same style as I did eight years ago. Out here we all were influenced by such men as Memoli and de Busscher, who used thin reeds and small-brilliant-toned oboes. Since these artists—and they *are* artists—have retired, and the dark "Eastern" players such as Bert Gassman have come into the fore in Los Angeles, we locally have had to conform with the change in tonal conception and alter our equipment to produce the dark mellow sound which has become the norm, rather than the exception. Hence, my reeds will probably resemble to some extent the Eastern type, i.e., long-scrape reeds as used by most of the Bloom and Tabuteau followers. I probably habitually use lighter reeds than, as an example, my old friend Ray Still of the Chicago Symphony. I have to use a lighter type reed because of the sort of playing I

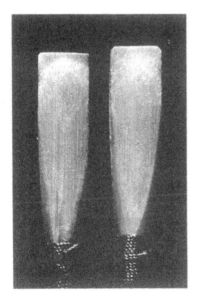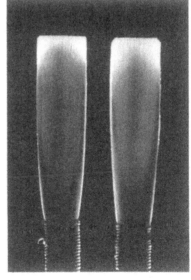

PLATE 73 The reeds of Gordon Schoneberg

have to do at Disney—a lot of rapid staccato passages, etc. When
I play a concert, I am inclined to use a somewhat heavier scrape.
The fact that I often have to play six or eight hours at a stretch
for several days with an eight-piece recording ensemble also tends
to make me want to work a little less hard with a resistant reed.

I admire the Tabuteau school of thought which turned out such
an abundance of great oboists and am sorry I did not have the
opportunity to study at Curtis in my younger years, but have
had to "make do" with what was available at the time. When I was
going to college, I even had to take oboe lessons privately. Of
course, things are much better locally, and they have fine woodwind departments at both U.S.C. and U.C.L.A.

The following is additional information from 1979:

Since Lym oboe number 89 I have owned at least 10 Rigoutat
oboes, 2 Rigoutat English horns, 2 Lorée oboes, and 1 Laubin
oboe. My reeds have changed many times over the years—being
influenced by the various instruments I have owned and by the
people I have performed with. The overall dimensions are about
68–70 mm on a 46 mm tube. They usually have a thin tip, some
thickness behind the tip, and usually some spine. They usually crow
high C. I have been using Gilbert's #1 shape lately. I gouge cane
to around 23 to 24 thousandths and try to use cane that I have had
in my possession for at least 5 years.

Dates of information: 1958, 1979.

Harry Shulman. Born December 15, 1915, in Rochester, New
York. Deceased 1965. In 1958 Shulman was First Oboist of the
American Broadcasting Company Orchestra. He had also been
First Oboist of the Pittsburgh Symphony and First Oboist of the
NBC Symphony. Shulman was a student of Marcel Tabuteau's.
He had also studied with Arthur Foreman and Mitchell Miller. He
played a Laubin oboe with serial number B 78.

Shulman was especially cognizant of the fact that an individual
designs reeds to suit factors such as the resistance, tone color, etc.
of his particular oboe. He believed that the important points of
reedmaking should be evaluated in the proper relation to the individual's instrument, embouchure, playing situation, and aural conception of the sound he wishes to achieve.

In 1952 Shulman wrote an article entitled "A Guide to a Flexible

Oboe: The Problem of Dark versus Bright Tone."[1] In that article he addressed the subject of tone coloration as being a problem for orchestral oboists, who are subjected to the opinions of many different conductors in regard to their tonal preferences for the many different styles of music. He recognizes that one cannot approach all music from the same tonal point of view. He sees the extremes of position in the sound rainbow as dark and thick on the one hand and brilliant and thin on the other. After pursuing this idea at some length he concludes that the moderately dark sound is the best point of departure as one searches for the aesthetic mean for each style. He believes that this sound holds the greatest possibilities for flexibility; that is, it allows for the greatest possibility for and facility in the change of sound coloration. Shulman states that, in essence, the sound of the individual oboist is the result of two factors: (1) the correlation between sound imagination and performance, and (2) the conception of the breathing chamber. It is of utmost importance that the air column extend down to the diaphragm. Shulman concludes, ". . . there is no need for the difficulties so inherent in the flexible situation of the present orchestral oboist. While preserving his integrity as a musician, he is still

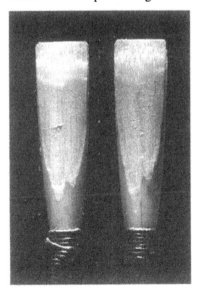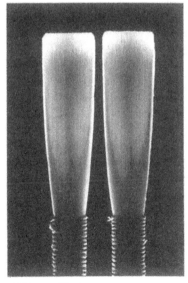

PLATE 74 The reeds of Harry Shulman

capable of conforming to the demands and tastes of the conductor or conductors he works with. This is one method which offers a reasonable solution."

Dates of information: 1958, 1980.

Robert Sprenkle. Born October 27, 1914, in Pittsburgh, Pennsylvania. Encouraged by his father to study music, Sprenkle took oboe lessons during his high school days, working with W. O. Schultz. After graduation—at which he was valedictorian—he continued lessons with Carlos Mullenix.

Sprenkle's first interest was engineering, however, and he was looking forward to a career in that field. A scholarship was waiting for him when he finished high school. But he took his oboe along when he went to Carnegie Institute, and, in the long run, music won out.

At the New England Music Camp in 1932, Sprenkle met Dr. Howard Hanson, who interested him in coming to the Eastman School of Music. Here he studied with Arthur Foreman and Robert Bloom. In 1936 he graduated with a B.M. and the performer's certificate, with honors, in oboe.

Joining the Rochester Philharmonic upon graduation, Sprenkle played English horn until his teacher, Robert Bloom, went to New York to become First Oboist in the newly organized NBC Symphony. At that time (1937) he was appointed principal of the oboe section—a position he has filled with great distinction ever since. At Eastman he teachers oboe and woodwind ensembles. Former students of Sprenkle are now playing in orchestras in Boston, New York, Washington, and other cities. He plays Lorée oboes AI 85 and BG 54.

Sprenkle has been soloist with the Rochester Philharmonic, the Civic Orchestra, the Eastman School Little Symphony, on the McCurdy Hour, and at Potsdam State Teachers College. He was featured as solo oboist in the recordings of Howard Hanson's *Pastorale*, Wayne Barlow's *The Winter's Passed*, the Loeffler Trio, the Barber *Capricorn Concerto*, and the Barlow Trio.

In 1979 Sprenkle made the following remarks regarding his reeds: "My reeds are substantially the same general style [as the 1958 examples in plate 75]. They have modest resistance (pressure range 8–16 oz.), crow about C but produce embouchure position notes from about G to D. They are tested to be responsive and

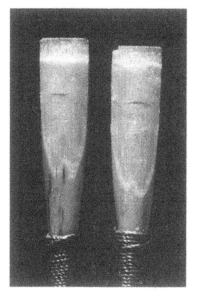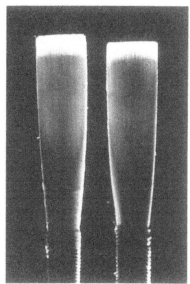

PLATE 75   The reeds of Robert Sprenkle

vibrant, but can be readily controlled by small lip and jaw adjustments while maintaining the desired pitch standard. The tubes are
45 mm and the total length is 67–69 mm with about .6 centimeter
at the tip."
    Dates of information: 1958, 1979.

Warren Stannard. Born September 4, 1923, in West Haven, Con-
necticut. At present (1979) Stannard plays English horn in the
Vancouver Symphony and teaches at the University of British
Columbia. Other positions that he has held include First Oboe,
Vancouver Symphony, 1960–76; First Oboe, CBC Vancouver
Chamber Orchestra, 1960–77; First Oboe, Indianapolis Symphony
Orchestra, 1953–60. He has also held positions as instructor of
oboe and theory at Oberlin Conservatory, Oberlin, Ohio, and Assistant Professor of Music at Colorado College. Stannard has studied with V. Caruso, C. Mullenix, Alvin Etler, and Ralph Gomberg.
In 1958 he played a Lorée oboe with serial number AL 61. He
presently plays Lorée oboe CK 45 and Lorée English horn CK 97
with a No. 1 Lorée bocal.
    In 1958 Stannard made the following remarks:

My oboe is quite low in pitch, and consequently, I must use a short tube—from 45 to 46 mm. I generally try to cut my reeds to 26 mm. I gouge my cane to .65 mm. in the center and about .45 mm. on the sides. I have been using cane imported from Longatte in Paris, and have no complaints about the quality.

You may notice a considerable difference in the two reeds I have sent. The one with my name on the tube [right-hand reed, both photographs, plate 76] was made before the season here, and the other, which is representative of the reeds I use with the symphony, is about what I like to use in the hall where we play.

Last summer, while in Connecticut, I found once again that my reeds made in the Midwest were quite bright and shrill in the East, although they were fine in Indianapolis. Conversely, the reeds made in the East were dull, dark, and unwieldy upon my return here. I think the higher the elevation, the longer the tip of the reed must be—for I noticed to a more marked degree the same phenomenon when I was in Colorado.

The following is from the year 1979:

I probably use a thinner scrape now-a-days—the fashion of oboe

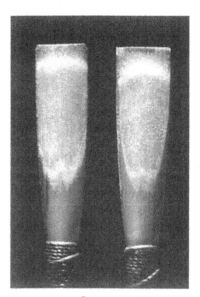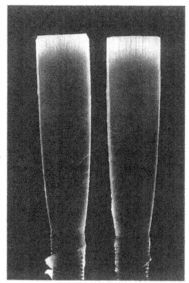

PLATE 76 The reeds of Warren Stannard

sound seems to have changed to a brighter quality. I still use the same gouge (±62 mm.) with a #C Prestini shape. As for English horn reeds, I use a medium gouge with a Brannon shape, the main virtue of which is that the bound reed doesn't leak! I prefer Lorée nickel silver tubes with both instruments.

Dates of information: 1958, 1979.

Ray Still. Born March 12, 1920. At the present time (1980) Still is First Oboist of the Chicago Symphony Orchestra. He has also been First Oboist of the Buffalo Philharmonic, First Oboist of the Baltimore Symphony Orchestra, and a member of the New York Woodwind Quintet. Still has studied with Fernand Gillet, Philip Memoli, and Robert Bloom. He considers Robert Bloom as the teacher who has had the greatest influence on his playing. Still plays a Lorée oboe with serial number AU 54.

Still stated in 1958 that his reeds are, in general, of the Tabuteau-Bloom school with some of the Sprenkle influence, which he as-similated through DeVere Moore. DeVere Moore was a student of Robert Sprenkle's and played English horn in the Baltimore Symphony when Still was First Oboist there.

The following remarks are made by Still:

The gouge is usually a little less than .60 mm. and the shape is a copy of one of Bloom's, which he got from Tabuteau—quite a simple one with very little noticeable belly (curvature) on the sides.

My aim is usually to try for the "C-crow," that is, C's an octave or two apart when the reed is held with too much of the cane part in the mouth, without much lip pressure, and blown quite hard.

I try for a minimum of resistance for blowing, consistent with a necessary "body" of sound. I try to hold the reed as near the tip as possible with the lips—the embouchure is puckered and the reed is allowed the maximum freedom to vibrate, hardly held at all at the *ff* level. It is held at a 45-degree angle, not at the low angle—that is, with the oboe held close to the body—used by many Eastman players. I try to get away from the extremes of the Tabuteau reed with its sharp drop-off from the "hump" to the tip. In other words—more graduation.

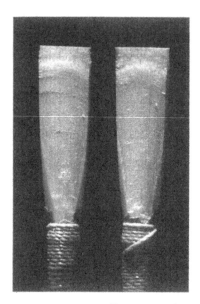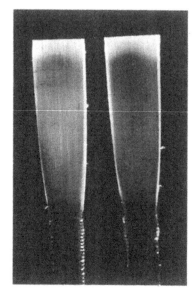

PLATE 77   The reeds of Ray Still

The reeds represented in plate 77 are both new ones and are fairly typical of the scrape that Still uses.

Dates of information: 1958, 1980.

Marcel Tabuteau (1887–1966). Born in Compiegne, France. Tabuteau left for Paris at the age of fourteen and won First Prize at the Paris Conservatory at age seventeen. The following year he came to the United States. Tabuteau played with the New York Symphony, was First Oboe with the Metropolitan Opera Orchestra, and was First Oboist of the Philadelphia Symphony Orchestra from 1915 until 1954. He was a member of the French Legion of Honor. He began teaching at the Curtis Institute of Music in Philadelphia in 1924, continuing to do so until his retirement in 1954. He moved to southern France after his retirement. He studied with Georges Gillet (1854–1934), who was Professor of Oboe at the Paris Conservatory from 1881 until 1929. He played Lorée oboes.

In this writer's opinion, Tabuteau has exerted a greater influence on oboe playing in this country than any other player, and his playing set a standard that will remain a goal for our finest players for years to come. It is through Tabuteau and his students that the "dark" tone has become so popular in the United States. This phenomenon has been like a chain reaction, influencing oboists all over the country, indeed, all over the world, by direct teaching, word of mouth, and recordings.

Tabuteau's conception of tone changed. When he first came to this country, he had the characteristic tone that was (and still is) preferred in France. He wanted to achieve a blend of the French tone with the dark and mellow qualities of the German oboe tone. He succeeded in doing this by what some oboists term the "long scrape," that is, by removing more bark from the back of the reed blades of the standard French cut and leaving more wood in the heart of the reed.

The third and fourth reeds in plate 78 look the way they should but are not good playing examples. The pitch is flat, of course, because the reeds are too long (see the reeds of Philip Kirchner and Tabuteau reeds 1 and 2 for better proportion and playing qualities of the same style reed). Tabuteau stated, "Remember, there are at least two kinds of reeds, the ones to be *played on* and the ones to be *looked at*." On the surface this remark might appear to be a witticism, but, like so many of Tabuteau's humorous remarks, this one also has the ring of truth when applied to many examples of oboe reeds. Almost all oboists have had reeds that looked terrible but played well.

Tabuteau maintained that the most important factor in the making of a reed is the gouge of the cane, not the *grattage*, or scratch. For the last few years before his retirement, he gouged tube cane from Var, which he selected while on several trips to the Prades Festival. After his retirement he continued to select and gouge tube cane from cane plantations in the areas of his several homes in the south of France. He used 10 to 10.5 millimeter cane tubes and gouged them about .57 millimeters to .59 millimeters thickness in the center. A thickness smaller than .55 millimeters or one greater than .60 millimeters was considered unusable. The gouge was graduated outward on both sides of the center to .55 millimeters, .50 millimeters, and .45 millimeters. However, this graduation was

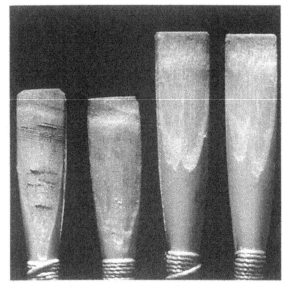

PLATE 78 The reeds of Marcel Tabuteau. Only
reeds 3 and 4 (counting from the left)
are shown in silhouette.

considered a variable factor, depending upon the setting of the
blade and the personal preference of the reedmaker.

It is difficult to describe the setting and shape of the gouge
blade. Tabuteau did his sharpening and shaping of the gouge blade
by hand on a hand grinder. He would then gouge a few pieces of
cane wet, measure them, and immediately make one or two reeds
to test the gouge—if it did not suit him he would grind and test
the blade until he was satisfied with the results.

There is an article by Laila Storch entitled "Marcel Tabuteau"
in *To the World's Oboists*, vol. II, no. 1, March 1974.

Dates of information: 1951–53, 1963–65.

Whitney Tustin. Born September 12, 1911, in Seattle, Washington. Tustin was First Oboist of the New York City Opera Company until 1966. He has also been associated with the Seattle Symphony Orchestra and the Kansas City Philharmonic. He is now

First Oboe of the Long Island Symphony and is on the faculty of Hofstra University and the Philadelphia College of Performing Arts. He has studied with Henri de Busscher in Los Angeles, Fernand Gillet in Boston, Messrs. Bajeux and Morel in Paris, and Leon Goossens in London. In 1958 he played a Lorée oboe with serial number Z 26. Presently he plays a Gordet oboe with serial number B 203.

The following paragraphs are paraphrased from an article Tustin wrote entitled "An Oboe Reed a Day."[2] He maintains that if one wishes to be a good oboist, he must spend an hour every day on reeds, usually in addition to (and after) his regular practicing.

He believes that we are frustrated many times in our search for the "perfect reed" because we tend to play for too long a period of time on an old favorite. He recommends that one try to get the best out of each new piece of cane, then adjust the embouchure and the style of playing to the result. One should try to avoid comparisons with the old reed.

Tustin maintains that a reed must satisfy all of the following points. It must (1) have a good tonal quality over the entire range, (2) have the right resistance, (3) have well-balanced intonation, and (4) feel comfortable to the player.

Tustin prefers to take a lot of time to make a reed and to break it in. He soaks the cane on one day. The next day he binds it on the stable and scrapes it until it crows freely. The day after that the reed will blow rather hard, so he scrapes it until it again crows freely. He repeats this process for a few days until he finds that the reeds have not changed from the day before. He then tries them on the oboe for tuning and the fine points of adjustment. He plays and adjusts them for a few minutes each day for several days until they are broken in. If, at this point, a reed shows weakness in any one of the points mentioned above, it is discarded immediately so that he will not become too attached to it.

In later correspondence Tustin states that he has not changed his ideas much since writing his article, but his ideas of what he wants the reed to sound like and how to achieve this sound are in constant experimentation. He remarks,

I find that through the years I constantly try for a darker sound (for me) compared with my beginning years, as this seems to sound better both in performance and in recording, is more controllable in *pp* in the lower notes, more stable in the upper notes, blends more easily with other woodwinds (especially flute), and is much easier on the embouchure.

During the past few years I have gotten started on a new line of thought which should have occurred to me a long time ago—namely, using a different type of reed depending on where it is to be played: in a small room with only several instruments or in an auditorium with a large group. Formerly, I used to try to play one reed for all occasions, until it commenced to get old and unresponsive. The result was, as I now look back, that my one reed was too strong for chamber music, needing too much control for volume, and it was too weak for orchestral work, and liable to lose its quality when forced. Nowadays, I know that if a reed plays well at home, it will be fine for sonata or chamber works, and I keep it for those purposes only. So then a reed which seems rather too thick and heavy, but, of course, well-balanced, at home will be just right during rehearsals and performances at the opera or in symphony concerts, especially when the audi-

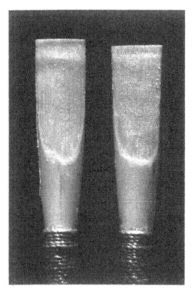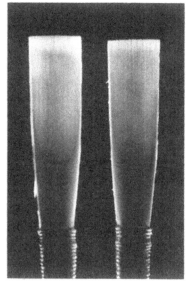

PLATE 79 The reeds of Whitney Tustin

toriums are filled. These heavier reeds I, of course, do not attempt to play elsewhere.

Tustin leaves gouging and shaping the cane preparatory to making reeds to the experts and gets the cane already gouged and folded. In 1958 he obtained cane from Irving Cohn, of Long Island, New York, and his average was ten or eleven good reeds out of every twelve pieces. This is an excellent average. Before his "retirement," he used from eight to ten reeds per year, but each reed represented at least twelve reeds that he made, tested, and finally rejected for some minor reason. In 1980 he uses "France" cane, shaped and folded, from Ponte Music Company, 142 West 46th Street, New York, New York 10036.

Dates of information: 1958, 1980.

Jean C. de Vergie. Born July 23, 1906, in Marseille, France. Deceased 1975. De Vergie was Second Oboist of the Boston Symphony Orchestra for over thirty-five years; prior to that time he was First Oboist of the Paris Opéra. His teachers were François

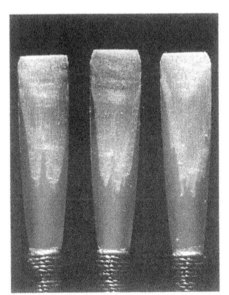
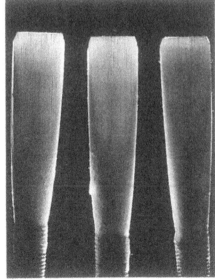

PLATE 80 The reeds of Jean de Vergie

Jean of the Marseille Conservatory and Louis Bleuzet of the Paris Conservatory. He was graduated from the Conservatory with First Prize. De Vergie played a Lorée oboe with serial number AL 69.

The reeds shown in plate 80 are of the kind he made for his pupils or on order. De Vergie stated that for the five years 1953–58 he had been using the reeds of Ralph Gomberg, the First Oboist of the Boston Symphony Orchestra, because he found that by using Gomberg's reeds their tones blended much better.

Dates of information: 1958, 1979.

Raymond S. Weaver, Jr. Born May 9, 1922, in Cumberland, Maryland. Weaver became First Oboist of the Houston Symphony in 1955. He joined the orchestra in 1950 and played for four years as Second Oboist. He began teaching at the University of Houston in 1951. He has done free-lance playing in motion picture studios, radio, the Los Angeles Chamber Symphony, and other organizations in the southern California area. In 1958 he played a Lorée oboe with serial number AR 5. He presently plays Lorée oboes CR 19 and CR 20.

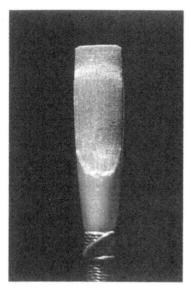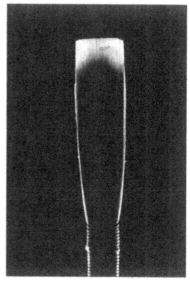

PLATE 81 A reed of Raymond Weaver, Jr.

The gouge of Weaver's cane is unique. It measures about .027 to .028 of an inch in the center when wet, thicker than average. It is fairly heavy on the edges, measuring .021 to .022 of an inch. He gouges the cane when it is *dry* because he believes that a much smoother gouge results, but, of course, one must then compensate in thickness for expansion when the cane is soaked for winding. Weaver favors fairly hard cane and seems to have a preference for nickel silver staples. The reed represented in plate 81 is one that he has played in concerts, and it has now about outlived its usefulness.

Dates of information: 1958, 1979.

Richard Woodhams. Born June 17, 1949, in Palo Alto, California. He joined the Philadelphia Orchestra as Principal Oboe in 1977. He was Principal Oboe of the St. Louis Symphony Orchestra from 1969 to 1977. In addition to many solo, chamber music, and festival appearances, he has been Principal Oboe and Main Instructor of Oboe at the Aspen Music Festival. He is a member of the Philadelphia Woodwind Quintet and an artist-teacher at Temple Uni-

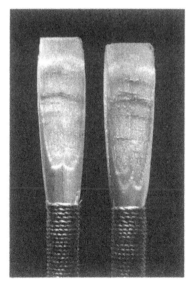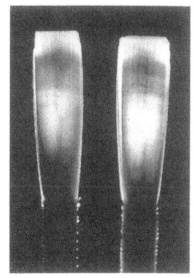

PLATE 82 The reeds of Richard Woodhams

versity College of Music. Woodhams studied with John de Lancie, John Mack, Robert Bloom, Jean-Louis Roux, Charles Price, and Raymond Duste. He plays Lorée oboe EE 35.

Woodhams remarks,

I strive in my reedmaking to create something with an optimum degree of resonance which will most effectively interact with the way in which I produce the sound and the acoustic environment in which I commonly play.

Therefore, my concept of a reed, as I am sure you will find true of most players, is based on a sensation of vibration that enables one to project a beautiful sound comfortably with secure pitch and as wide a range of dynamics as possible, avoiding both the shallowness of quality associated with too easy a reed and the lack of malleability inherent in blowing something with excessive resistance.

I don't think it is possible to understand much about a reed by looking at it, as the quality of a reed is mostly determined by factors other than its actual scrape. I played five performances of the Strauss Oboe Concerto on the green one [left-hand reed in both photographs of plate 82], and the red one I picked up off my desk.

Date of information: 1980.

8

A Delineation of Reed Styles

SCHOOLS OF PLAYING are recognizable when players, usually of a given time and/or place, demonstrate a similarity of tone quality and style of playing that can be related to guiding principles and methods that they (consciously or unconsciously) employ. That is, players who have similar aural conceptions, breathing methods, and embouchures, who use instruments with like characteristics, who play in much the same musical situation, and who therefore cut their reeds on the same general pattern tend to fall into distinguishable groups. As these similar conceptions become more widely accepted, we may delineate, compare, and contrast various areas of stylistic usage. Of course, there will be differences in the technical and tonal results of individual players, but the principles used will be basically the same.

After a school is established, it tends to breed players imbued with the stylistic principles to which it adheres. The situation is familiar to all whereby ideas, techniques, and principles of tone production, reedmaking, and musical phrasing are propagated from teacher to students over the years. In the preceding chapters these principles and methods have been discussed under general headings of tone production and technique. They have been shown to

167

be interrelated perhaps more than they are usually thought to be. Now the function of the reed may be placed in better perspective.

The writer feels that his experience and the results of this study indicate the following premises:

1. The scrape of a given oboist's reed is dependent upon the method of tone production (breathing, embouchure, etc.), the instrument, the teacher, and the aural concept of the player.

2. The scrape of a player's reed will dictate in large part the results he will get in articulation, dynamics, tone quality, and the amount of musical control he can effect.

3. The opposite may also be true; that is, the results the player desires in articulation, dynamics, tone quality, and amount of musical control will in large part dictate the scrape of the reed.

Principles of reedmaking (manifested in the measurements of Table 3) have evolved as the result of a desire on the part of the player for a certain timbre—born of a personal aural concept, sometimes influenced by the listener—and a desire, indeed, a necessity, to facilitate a technique adequate enough to enable the player to express himself musically, according to his musical taste.

The preceding photographs of reeds in chapter 7 and Tables 3–14 to come in chapter 9 suggest that if the field of reedmaking is considered as a spectrum from extremely short scrape to extremely long scrape, certain definable areas can be marked off as characteristic of the way a number of players make reeds. These areas—or styles—reflect a grouping of a number of similar cases determined by their measurements. Table 5, *Length of Scrape*, demonstrates that the statistical evidence supports the existence of a shorter and a longer scrape reed. The visual similarities of styles are also readily apparent, and reeds that resemble one another visually also have strong audible similarities when compared by actual playing.

These definable styles do bear out in actual sound at least one thing that the writer believed before making the study—namely, that the timbre of a reed is changed (all other aspects of playing remaining equal) in direct proportion to the amount of wood removed from the tip, lay, and back of the blades of the reed.

Because the spectrum of reed sound is continuous, styles overlap, so that we come up with borderline examples. Borderline examples are difficult to categorize, so the writer has defined only those areas which are obvious.

In the pages that follow the reader will note that five definite styles of reeds (French, American, Dutch, Viennese, English) and one borderline style (German) are clearly definable.

THE FRENCH-STYLE REED

This type of reed has probably had more influence than any other in the history of the true French oboe. All of the examples and photographs of oboe reeds from other historical periods that the writer has seen bear testimony to this fact.[1] Today this style of reed lives on strongly, especially in Europe, either as the true French-style reed or only slightly modified, as in the case of the Italian examples. There appears to be no appreciable difference in measurement that can substantiate the existence of a true "Italian" style. Perhaps the opportunity to survey more examples would serve to establish an "Italian" style, but in the writer's opinion at this time, it is unlikely, since the Italian reeds he has studied are valid examples from excellent, representative Italian oboists.

The greatest deviations from the French style are the Russian reeds of Petrov; the Viennese reeds of ca. 1800 still extant in the examples of Kamesch, Kautzky, and Raab;[2] the Dutch reeds of Houttuin and Stotijn; and the long-scrape American type of ca. 1907. The writer finds it difficult to say whether the short, swallow-tailed reeds of Petrov and Kamesch actually derived from the narrower French reed or rather followed their own line down from the more primitive shawm reed.[3] The long-scrape American reed is a derivative of the French style.

The writer hesitates to select one typical example of a true French-style reed, preferring to let the reader see several examples that fall within this category. The reeds of Duvoir (plate 51), however, come close to being a typical example. The reed of Bleuzet (plate 24), even though a bit worn, is truly French, coming as it does from the fountainhead of French oboe playing, the Paris Conservatory, and from one of the greatest French oboists. The reeds of Claro (plate 26) and Dandois (plate 50) and Reed 1 of Rizzo (plate 69) are good examples of the French reed.

The French-style reed is characterized by an overall length of around 72 millimeters, a short scrape (9–13 millimeters) with its attendant long lay, and no rind removed from the back of the reed.[4]

Numerous recordings of French soloists (notably Pierlot) and wind groups give a representative sample of the French oboe sound.

THE AMERICAN-STYLE REED

Plate 78 shows the reeds of Tabuteau. The American-style reed (the writer uses this name because it seems to be in rather wide use and also because there seems to be no better one) is, of course, a modification of the French and was brought about as a direct result of the reedmaking, teaching, and experimentation of Marcel Tabuteau during the first and second decades of this century. This style of reed has become predominant in the United States in the last thirty to forty years because most of the older, French-style oboists have retired from the professional orchestras of this country, and most of the younger players prefer the sound given by the longer-scrape reed. The reader will notice in the biographies of players from the United States that Tabuteau had many fine students and they, of course, helped propagate his style of reedmaking and playing. There are many other examples of "typical" American reeds. Some of the most obvious are those of Angelucci (plate 42), Bloom (plate 45), Harold Gomberg (plate 55), Kirchner (plate 58), Lifschey (plate 60), Mack (plate 61), Mariotti (plate 62), Sprenkle (plate 75), and Still (plate 77). As he studies all the American examples, the reader will note that there are variations from a central tendency in this reed style, as in the other styles, which serve to join the several international reed styles into a continuous spectrum. Numerous recordings of the American sound are available, notably those of the New York Philharmonic, the Philadelphia, Chicago, Los Angeles, Rochester, St. Louis, and Cleveland symphony orchestras, and the solo recordings of Marcel Tabuteau, Harold Gomberg, and Robert Sprenkle.

The American-type reed is characterized by the long scrape (14–22 millimeters) with the attendant thicker heart. The tip and lay are rather short, and the rind is removed in varying amounts from the back. The overall length is generally shorter than that of the French style to compensate for the flatness caused by scraping the back so much. Aside from the length of scrape, the writer finds no significant differences between the long and short scrape types in thickness of gouge and all the other measurements in Table 3.

THE ENGLISH-STYLE REED

Of the English examples, it is apparent that those of Baker (plate 10), Jones (plate 14), Newbury (plate 17), Tait (plate 20), and Wickens (plate 21), have much in common, perhaps through the quite considerable legacy of Brierly (plate 11). If there is a definable trend or style in England, it is probably manifested in reeds of this type. The writer believes that a good case might be made for an English style represented by the above examples and characterized by a slightly shorter scrape (9 millimeters) and thinner lay than the present-day French style. The reeds of Lord (plate 15) and MacDonagh (plate 16) are slightly darker in sound, and those of Craxton (plate 12), Graeme (plate 13), Rothwell (plate 18), and Sutcliffe (plate 19) are long-scrape reeds.

THE DUTCH-STYLE REED

The Dutch-style reed is a clearly definable one and is used in conjunction with the Dutch-type embouchure. The reeds of Stotijn (plate 34) are typical, as are those of Houttuin (plate 32) and Pels (plate 33).

These reeds are necessarily shorter in overall dimensions, because the thick gouge (.030–.037 inch), the long tip, lay (12–16 millimeters), and back, and the wide shape (7.05–8.00 millimeters) tend toward flatness of pitch. They sound (speak) under comparatively small wind pressure because the reeds have little resistance.

THE VIENNESE-STYLE REED

These reeds are made to be played on the Viennese large-bore oboe and are limited to that area of Europe around Vienna. Examples of the Viennese reed are those of Kamesch (plate 3), Kautzky (plate 4), and Raab (plate 6). One could possibly put the Russian reed of Petrov (plate 40) and the Leningrad example (plate 39) in this category because of noticeable similarities.

These reeds have a short staple (37–38 millimeters), a long tip and back (15–16 millimeters), and a swallow-tailed shape (7.25–7.55 millimeters width at widest point). The resistance is light and the tone pleasant. Kamesch made several recordings that give a representation of this sound. A point of interest is the almost perfect circle of the small end of the staple, which is usually oval. In the writer's opinion, this style of reed is very close to the baroque reed, pointing up the fact that the baroque oboe sound was a *refined* sound in comparison to, for example, the Catalan shawm tone, which is still in existence in northern Spain. The shawm tone is a wild and exciting sound but certainly does not fit our musical concept of the courtly halls of Louis XIV and the charming ballets of Lully.

A BORDERLINE STYLE

It is possible to define one additional, less obvious style of reed, which is a combination of the short-scrape (French) and long-scrape (American) styles. Many of the same features of the *German* reed of Eggers (plate 27) are duplicated, to varying degrees, in those of Fischer (plate 28), Töttcher (plate 31), Kalmus (plate 29), Schlövogt (plate 30), Hanták (plate 8), and Duchoň (plate 7). The reeds of Woolley (plate 2), Tancibudek (plate 1), and Booth (plate 38), are also the same general German style, but of slightly different proportion. All of these reeds have a longer scrape than the French, but a shorter one than the American. They have the noticeable heart in the center of the lay.

The examples from Italy (previously noted) and Switzerland follow the French so closely that the reeds are practically identical as to their central tendencies. Because there are slight differences in aural concept, however, the writer can only surmise that the different sounds achieved on these reeds are in large part due to the way they are played and not to the basic cut of the reed.

Now, as to national tendencies, American-style reeds predominate among the oboists of the United States, with some French-style reeds in use.

Sipila (plate 22) in Finland modifies toward the American style rather than the French. Wolsing (plate 9) in Denmark makes what is basically an American-style reed, perhaps because of his study with Tabuteau.

In France the examples show a predominate French style with only a modification toward a longer scrape by some of the younger players.

The German reeds fall proportionately in the area of the short to midrange scrape; they also tend to be somewhat narrower in width.

From Australia the reeds of Woolley and Booth seem to be more "English," while those of Tancibudek and the Czechs, Hanták and Duchoň, may be more akin to the German reeds (or the German ones more akin to theirs).

As has been pointed out, the Swiss and the Italians use the same general style as the French.

There is also a cutting across of national boundaries in some cases such as Lardrot (plate 5), once in Austria and now in Switzerland.

In summary, we have seen that five basic styles (French, American, English, Dutch, and Viennese) can be delineated. It would be difficult and perhaps presumptuous to place the borderline German cases in a definite style category, partly because of the rather limited examples that the writer has observed. However, the German reeds are considered to have characteristics different enough to set them apart from the five clearly definable styles. Further study of an expanded number of observable examples would likely confirm that they are more than just borderline cases.

9
Summary and Conclusions

IN CHAPTER 7 there are photographs of 168 examples of reeds from 81 reedmakers of 14 countries. Table 3 lists the dimensions of these 168 reeds in alphabetical order by country and player.

The writer fails to find any appreciable difference between the dimensions of French-, American-, and English-type reeds except in length of scrape and amount of rind removed from behind the lay. Other dimensional variations fall within the same range and many of them are, no doubt, nullified (or compensated for) by individual methods of tone production, embouchure, and instruments of separate players. Noticeable visual differences are, of course, reflected in the measurements.

On the other hand, one finds that distinctly noticeable dimensional differences exist in almost every area when one compares the Dutch and Viennese with the French, American, and English styles.

One can make some interesting statistical observations based on Table 3, Table of Reed Measurements. Tables 4–14 are simple mathematical interpretations of each column of Table 3. The writer's observations accompany those tables in an attempt to clarify and interpret the figures presented.

The following notes will aid in interpreting Table 3.

174

Reeds marked, for example, "ex Sutcliffe" are reeds that were given or loaned to the writer by that oboist.

All measurements are in millimeters. A great majority of the measurements can be made with a millimeter scale, a micrometer calibrated in hundredths of a millimeter with a slightly rounded spindle, a dial indicator mounted with feeler (see plate 65), and a small hole gage. The measurements for columns 8, 9, 10, and 12 can be somewhat grossly approximated with a millimeter scale. However, the measurements presented in these columns were made on an electronic instrument that would normally be found in a large machine shop or physics laboratory, and they have a rather high degree of accuracy.

For several reasons, one of which was that the measuring instruments were calibrated in the English system, the measurements for columns 1, 3, and 12 were originally made in thousandths of an inch. To maintain consistency in Table 3, these measurements have been converted to the metric system. The following tables reconvert metric to English for columns 1, 3, and 12. The reader will note occasional compromises between the two systems; however, they are of little consequence because they are so small.

For column 1, Center Thickness of Gouge

Millimeters	Inches	Millimeters	Inches
.94	.037	.68	.027
.91	.036	.66	.026
.89	.035	.63	.025
.86	.034	.61	.024
.84	.033	.58	.023
.81	.032	.56	.022
.79	.031	.53	.021
.76	.030	.51	.020
.74	.029	.48	.019
.71	.028	.46	.018

For column 3, Tip Thickness

Millimeters	Inches	Millimeters	Inches
.01	.0005	.13	.0050
.02	.0010	.14	.0055
.04	.0015	.15	.0060
.05	.0020	.17	.0065
.07	.0025	.18	.0070

Millimeters	Inches	Millimeters	Inches
.08	.0030	.19	.0075
.09	.0035	.20	.0080
.10	.0040	.22	.0085
.11	.0045	.23	.0090

For column 12, Staple Material Thickness

Millimeters	Inches	Millimeters	Inches
.43	.017	.28	.011
.41	.016	.25	.010
.38	.015	.23	.009
.36	.014	.20	.008
.33	.013	.18	.007
.30	.012		

The measurements in column 3 were made at the L(eft), C(enter), and R(ight) points on Blade 1 and at the opposing points (that is, R, C, and L) on Blade 2.

In column 8 the measurement is across the inside diameter (I.D.) of the base of the staple.

In column 9 the measurement is of the inside diameter of the top of the staple across the long axis of the ellipse.

In column 10 the measurement is of the inside diameter of the top of the staple across the short axis of the ellipse.

An important point to notice in columns 9 and 10 is to what degree the top of the staple is either oval or elliptical.

In column 11, *B* stands for brass; *NS* stands for nickel silver.

TABLE 3
Table of Reed Measurements
All measurements in millimeters

Name	Reed No.	1 Center Thickness of Gouge	2 Length of Scrape	3 Tip Thickness Blade 1 L	3 Blade 1 C	3 Blade 1 R	3 Blade 2 Opposing		4 Cane Width, Widest Point	5 Cane Length, Binding to Tip	6 Overall Length of Reed	7 Staple Length	8 Staple Dim. at Base, I.D.	9 Staple Dim. at Top, Long Axis of Ellipse, I.D.	10 Staple Dim. at Top, Short Axis of Ellipse, I.D.	11 Staple Material	12 Staple Material Thickness
AUSTRALIA																	
Jiri Tancibudek	1	.63	16.0	.05	.11	.02	.05	.13 .02	6.75	25.0	72.0	47.0	4.83	2.50	1.90	B	.36
	2	.51	14.0	.05	.10	.05	.05	.11 .05	6.57	25.0	74.0	49.0	5.00	2.60	1.95	B	.30
David L. T. Woolley	1	.63	12.5	.02	.04	.02	.04	.08 .04	6.85	27.0	72.0	45.0	4.66	2.50	1.90	B	.36
	2	.63	12.5	.05	.08	.04	.05	.08 .04	6.92	27.5	72.5	45.0	4.82	2.70	1.95	B	.30
AUSTRIA																	
Hans Kamesch	1	.56	15.0	.02	.01	.01	.01	.01 .01	7.42	23.0	62.0	37.0	4.90	2.85	1.95	B	.36
	2	.56	15.0	.01	.01	.02	.01	.01 .01	7.45	24.0	61.0	37.0	4.90	2.70	1.95	B	.36
Manfred Kautzky	1	.56	15.5	.01	.01	.01	.01	.01 .01	7.25	25.0	62.0	37.0	4.90	2.70	2.05	B	.38
	2	.53	15.5	.02	.02	.02	.02	.02 .01	7.25	25.0	62.0	37.0	4.94	2.65	2.15	B	.43
André Lardrot	1	.74	10.0	.01	.05	.01	.04	.08 .01	7.00	28.0	76.0	47.0	4.87	2.70	1.90	B	.30
	2	.58	10.0	.05	.10	.02	.02	.08 .02	7.00	28.0	76.0	47.0	4.88	2.80	1.90	B	.30
Ferdinand Raab	1	.53	16.0	.05	.10	.08	.05	.10 .07	7.55	25.0	63.0	38.0	4.90	2.85	1.90	B	.23
	2	.56	16.0	.01	.09	.07	.02	.07 .05	7.47	25.0	63.0	38.0	5.00	2.90	2.20	B	.23
CZECHOSLOVAKIA																	
Stanislav Duchoň	1	.46	10.5	.02	.05	.02	.02	.05 .02	6.10	23.5	70.0	46.5	4.68	2.55	2.10	B	.20
	2	.48	10.5	.01	.04	.01	.01	.04 .01	6.15	23.0	68.0	45.0	4.63	2.60	2.10	B	.23
František Hanták	1	.66	11.0	.01	.02	.02	.01	.05 .01	6.87	25.0	70.0	46.0	4.77	2.65	1.90	B	.20
	2	.56	11.0	.01	.04	.04	.01	.04 .02	6.75	25.0	71.0	46.0	4.67	2.50	1.85	B	.23
	3	.56	10.0	.01	.02	.01	.01	.02 .01	6.50	24.0	71.0	46.0	4.67	2.70	2.15	B	.25
DENMARK																	
Waldemar Wolsing	1	.58	19.0	.01	.04	.02	.02	.02 .02	7.50	23.5	70.5	47.0	4.87	2.70	1.80	NS	.41
	2	.58	19.0	.02	.04	.02	.02	.04 .02	6.90	23.5	70.5	47.0	4.89	2.60	2.00	NS	.36
ENGLAND																	
Harry Baker	1	.56	9.0	.01	.01	.02	.01	.01 .01	6.80	23.5	71.0	47.0	4.86	3.10	1.70	B	.28
	2	.53	9.0	.01	.01	.01	.01	.01 .01	6.80	23.5	71.0	47.0	4.81	3.80	1.85	B	.28

TABLE 3 *(continued)*

Name	Reed No.	1 Center Thickness of Gouge	2 Length of Scrape	3 Tip Thickness Blade 1 L	C	R	Blade 2 Opposing		4 Cane Width, Widest Point	5 Cane Length, Binding to Tip	6 Overall Length of Reed	7 Staple Length	8 Staple Dim. at Base, I.D.	9 Staple Dim. at Top, Long Axis of Ellipse, I.D.	10 Staple Dim. at Top, Short Axis of Ellipse, I.D.	11 Staple Material	12 Staple Material Thickness
ENGLAND *continued*																	
Thomas Brierly (ex Brain, Sutcliffe)	1	.58	9.0	.02	.05	.04	.02 .05	.05	6.75	26.0	69.0	43.0	4.62	2.90	1.90	B	.33
	2	.53	8.0	.02	.05	.08	.05 .10	.10	6.90	25.5	74.0	47.0	4.97	2.80	1.80	B	.30
Janet Craxton	1	.58	15.0	.07	.05	.08	.10 .05	.10	6.85	22.5	65.5	43.0	4.47	2.85	1.95	B	.30
	2	.61	15.0	.02	.05	.04	.05 .08	.08	6.80	22.5	68.0	45.5	4.77	2.80	2.05	B	.30
Peter Graeme	1	.61	14.0	.02	.05	.05	.05 .05	.04	6.62	24.0	71.0	47.0	4.81	2.70	2.10	B	.28
	2	.58	13.0	.05	.08	.02	.05 .08	.05	6.65	24.0	71.0	47.0	4.85	2.80	1.90	B	.30
Tom Jones	1	.53	9.0	.02	.05	.04	.02 .02	.02	6.87	25.5	73.0	47.0	4.85	2.80	1.90	B	.30
	2	.53	9.0	.05	.09	.15	.08 .08	.08	7.10	25.5	73.0	47.0	4.95	2.90	1.95	B	.30
Roger Lord	1	.58	10.0	.05	.07	.08	.05 .08	.05	6.70	26.0	72.0	46.0	4.78	2.85	1.80	B	.33
	2	.51	11.0	.08	.09	.07	.05 .08	.05	6.60	25.0	71.0	46.0	4.73	2.55	1.80	B	.38
Terence MacDonagh	1	.61	10.0	.02	.08	.01	.05 .08	.05	6.60	24.0	71.0	47.0	4.68	2.60	1.75	B	.28
	2	.58	10.0	.02	.05	.02	.04 .08	.05	6.90	25.0	72.0	47.0	4.82	2.65	1.75	B	.36
Peter Newbury	1	.61	9.0	.02	.02	.01	.01 .01	.01	6.50	24.0	72.0	48.0	4.82	3.10	1.75	B	.30
	2	.61	9.0	.01	.01	.01	.01 .02	.01	6.70	23.0	72.0	49.0	5.07	2.70	1.85	B	.25
Evelyn Rothwell	1	.61	15.0	.01	.01	.01	.01 .01	.01	6.80	23.0	70.5	47.5	4.87	2.85	1.95	B	.30
	2	.63	15.0	.02	.01	.04	.02 .05	.01	6.60	24.0	71.0	47.0	4.89	2.95	1.95	NS	.30
Sidney Sutcliffe	1	.63	17.0	.02	.05	.02	.02 .08	.05	6.75	25.5	65.5	40.0	4.73	2.85	2.15	B	.28
	2	.63	18.0	.05	.14	.08	.08 .15	.13	6.80	25.0	71.0	46.0	4.88	2.80	1.95	NS	.30
William Tait	1	.58	9.0	.04	.04	.02	.04 .05	.04	6.85	25.5	68.0	42.5	4.34	3.50	3.05	B	.23
Derek Wickens	1	.76	9.0	.01	.04	.02	.02 .04	.04	7.18	26.0	73.5	47.0	4.83	2.85	1.90	B	.30
	2	.63	9.0	.02	.02	.01	.05 .05	.04	7.18	26.0	73.5	47.0	4.86	2.90	1.95	B	.30
FINLAND																	
Asser Sipila	1	.63	14.0	.02	.05	.07	.10 .10	.13	6.75	26.5	75.0	48.0	4.82	2.95	1.70	B	.25
	2	.63	14.0	.05	.05	.09	.08 .09	.08	6.85	26.5	73.5	47.0	4.80	2.60	1.85	B	.33

FRANCE																		
Pierre Bajeux (ex Craxton)	1	.61	9.0	.01	.04	.01	.02	.05	.01	6.80	26.0	73.0	47.0	4.78	2.75	2.10	B	.30
L. F. A. Bleuzet (ex Wolsing)	1	.68	12.0*	.08	.08	.08	.08	.08	.08	6.85	27.5	75.0	47.0	4.89	2.90	2.00	B	.30
André Chevalet	1	.58	12.0	.02	.05	.02	.04	.05	.02	6.80	25.0	72.0	47.0	4.85	2.65	1.50	B	.28
	2	.58	13.0	.04	.02	.02	.01	.01	.01	7.10	25.0	72.0	47.0	4.91	2.80	1.50	B	.30
Raymond Claro	1	.61	12.0	.01	.01	.01	.01	.01	.01	6.82	27.0	74.0	47.0	4.82	2.65	1.80	B	.28
	2	.61	10.0	.01	.02	.01	.01	.01	.01	6.87	26.0	73.0	47.0	4.98	2.45	1.85	B	.28
	3	.58	10.0	.01	.01	.01	.01	.01	.01	7.02	26.0	73.0	47.0	4.83	2.85	1.80	B	.30
GERMANY																		
Helmut Eggers	1	.61	11.0	.08	.10	.05	.08	.11	.07	6.40	25.0	73.0	48.0	4.71	2.90	1.90	B	.30
	2	.61	10.0	.02	.07	.01	.05	.13	.04	6.60	24.0	72.0	48.0	4.67	2.70	1.85	B	.30
Fritz Fischer	1	.56	10.5	.01	.08	.02	.01	.08	.02	6.65	27.0	73.5	47.0	4.67	2.75	2.10	B	.28
	2	.58	10.5	.02	.08	.02	.01	.08	.02	6.55	26.5	73.0	47.0	4.67	2.70	2.00	B	.28
Kurt Kalmus	1	.71	13.0	.04	.08	.05	.01	.09	.02	8.20	27.5	67.5	40.0	4.37	2.90	2.20	B	.25
	2	.63	11.5	.02	.08	.08	.05	.13	.05	8.12	26.5	68.5	42.0	4.45	2.60	2.10	B	.30
	3	.68	12.0	.04	.09	.04	.05	.08	.02	8.20	26.0	69.0	43.0	4.63	2.60	2.10	B	.20
Helmut Schlövogt	1	.56	10.5	.02	.04	.02	.01	.02	.01	6.55	25.0	72.0	47.0	4.72	2.60	1.95	B	.28
	2	.58	10.5	.01	.02	.02	.01	.02	.02	6.57	25.0	72.0	47.0	4.65	2.70	1.85	B	.28
Hermann Törtcher	1	.56	9.0	.02	.08	.02	.02	.08	.04	6.95	25.0	73.0	48.0	4.48	2.80	2.15	B	.36
	2	.56	9.0	.05	.10	.02	.05	.08	.02	6.95	25.0	73.0	48.0	4.55	2.60	2.10	B	.36
HOLLAND																		
Simon Houtrin	1	.81	16.0	.02	.13	.09	.08	.08	.04	7.05	23.0	64.0	41.0	4.86	2.65	1.85	B	.28
	2	.76	17.0	.15	.15	.09	.11	.10	.07	7.25	26.0	67.0	41.0	4.94	2.70	2.00	B	.28
Ferdinand Pels	1	.79	14.0	.01	.05	.01	.01	.01	.05	7.00	25.5	68.5	42.5	4.83	2.80	2.10	B	.30
	2	.81	12.0	.01	.07	.04	.01	.05	.05	7.30	25.0	67.5	42.5	4.53	2.80	2.15	B	.30
Jaap Stotijn	1	.94	12.0	.02	.05	.09	.02	.05	.09	8.00	28.0	66.0	38.0	4.82	2.90	2.20	B	.25
	2	.94	12.0	.01	.01	.02	.01	.01	.01	7.80	28.0	65.0	37.0	4.57	3.00	2.20	B	.30
ITALY																		
Tullio Riedmiller	1	.56	10.0	.05	.07	.01	.04	.05	.01	6.85	26.0	73.0	47.0	4.77	2.75	2.00	NS	.38
	2	.56	10.0	.04	.04	.01	.01	.02	.01	6.75	25.0	73.0	47.0	4.64	2.55	2.15	NS	.38
	3	.58	10.0	.01	.02	.01	.01	.05	.01	6.80	25.5	72.0	47.0	4.64	2.75	2.10	NS	.38

Tip lost

TABLE 3 *(continued)*

Name	Reed No.	1 Center Thickness of Gouge	2 Length of Scrape	3 Tip Thickness Blade 1 L	C	R	3 Tip Thickness Blade 2 Opposing			4 Cane Width, Widest Point	5 Cane Length, Binding to Tip	6 Overall Length of Reed	7 Staple Length	8 Staple Dim. at Base, I.D.	9 Staple Dim. at Top, Long Axis of Ellipse, I.D.	10 Staple Dim. at Top, Short Axis of Ellipse, I.D.	11 Staple Material	12 Staple Material Thickness
ITALY *continued*																		
Federico de Sanctis	1	.58	10.0	.05	.10	.05	.05	.10	.02	7.30	25.0	73.0	48.0	4.67	2.70	2.20	NS	.28
	2	.58	9.5	.05	.13	.08	.02	.09	.02	7.03	25.0	72.0	47.0	4.82	2.70	2.05	NS	.30
Giuseppe Tomassini	1	.53	11.0	.05	.05	.02	.02	.02	.01	6.90	25.0	74.0	49.0	4.86	2.80	1.90	B	.36
	2	.58	10.0	.04	.07	.04	.01	.04	.01	7.10	25.0	73.0	48.0	4.81	2.55	1.95	B	.33
NEW ZEALAND																		
Norman Edwin Booth	1	.56	10.0	.08	.07	.04	.05	.08	.08	6.80	23.5	72.5	49.0	4.95	2.70	1.95	B	.28
	2	.61	11.0	.05	.04	.04	.04	.05	.02	6.67	23.5	71.5	48.0	4.84	2.70	1.85	B	.28
RUSSIA																		
Leningrad Sym. (ex Sutcliffe)	1	.56	10.0	.10	.08	.05	.04	.08	.08	7.00	25.0	71.0	47.5	4.68	2.50	2.50	B	.28
Anatol Petrov	1	.56	15.0	.02	.04	.02	.05	.09	.05	7.50	22.0	58.0	21.0	4.77	1.85	1.65	B	.33
	2	.56	16.0	.04	.07	.04	.04	.07	.07	7.53	22.0	59.5	22.5	4.73	2.80	2.05	B	.30
SWITZERLAND																		
Egon Parolari	1	.58	10.0	.01	.02	.01	.02	.04	.02	7.45	27.0	74.0	47.0	4.96	2.80	1.90	B	.28
	2	.58	11.0	.04	.08	.08	.08	.07	.07	7.30	27.0	73.5	42.5	4.82	2.75	1.70	B	.28
UNITED STATES																		
Rhadames Angelucci	1	.63	21.0	.01	.02	.01	.01	.04	.01	7.15	23.0	73.0	48.0	5.00	2.85	1.75	B	.28
	2	.61	22.0	.01	.02	.02	.05	.08	.04	7.15	23.5	70.0	47.0	4.75	2.85	1.80	B	.33
Leonard Arner	1	.56	18.0	.02	.05	.02	.01	.02	.02	7.00	24.0	72.0	48.0	4.95	2.80	1.90	B	.28
	2	.56	18.0	.05	.05	.02	.05	.05	.05	6.82	24.5	72.5	48.0	4.91	2.90	1.80	B	.28
Alfred Barthel	1	.46	7.0*	.20	.20	.20	.23	.23	.20	6.75	25.0	72.5	47.5	4.78	2.80	2.00	B	.30
Robert Bloom	1	.61	20.0	.01	.01	.01	.01	.01	.01	6.62	24.0	71.0	47.0	4.88	2.91	1.89	NS	.28
	2	.61	20.0	.01	.01	.01	.01	.01	.01	6.65	24.0	70.5	47.0	4.88	2.77	2.06	NS	.23

Name	#																	
Peter Bowman	1	.63	18.5	.01	.01	.01	.01	.01	.01	6.86	21.5	69.0	47.0	4.98	2.79	2.02	NS	.23
	2	.58	18.5	.01	.01	.01	.01	.01	.01	6.85	21.5	69.5	48.0	4.88	2.72	1.92	NS	.25
Henri de Busscher	1	.61	14.0	.01	.04	.01	.01	.04	.01	7.25	24.5	69.5	46.0	4.67	2.80	1.90	B	.30
	2	.61	16.0	.01	.01	.04	.01	.01	.01	7.25	23.5	70.5	47.0	4.87	2.85	1.95	B	.28
James Caldwell	1	.61	18.0	.01	.01	.01	.01	.01	.01	6.75	21.5	68.0	47.0	4.91	2.78	1.70	NS	.33
	2	.61	18.5	.01	.01	.01	.01	.01	.01	6.80	22.0	68.5	47.0	4.84	2.91	1.90	NS	.20
Liliane Lhoest Covington	1	.68	16.0	.02	.05	.07	.02	.07	.01	6.75	24.5	70.5	46.0	4.89	2.75	1.90	B	.20
	2	.63	16.0	.07	.09	.07	.07	.07	.01	6.60	25.0	72.0	47.0	5.12	2.30	1.70	B	.18
Marcel Dandois	1	.63	11.0	.01	.07	.07	.04	.07	.02	7.05	28.0	75.0	47.0	4.87	2.85	1.80	B	.28
	2	.61	11.0	.01	.05	.07	.01	.05	.01	6.96	27.0	74.0	47.0	4.87	2.80	1.80	B	.28
	3	.61	11.0	.02	.07	.05	.02	.05	.01	6.90	26.0	73.0	47.0	4.94	2.80	1.90	B	.25
	4	.56	8.0	.08	.08	.10	.08	.10	.01	6.80	26.0	74.0	47.0	4.87	2.80	1.80	B	.28
Alexandre Duvoir	1	.61	10.0	.01	.04	.04	.01	.04	.01	7.45	27.0	75.0	48.0	4.86	2.75	1.85	B	.28
	2	.63	10.0	.01	.04	.04	.05	.04	.05	7.20	27.0	75.0	48.0	4.82	2.85	1.90	B	.30
Bert Gassman	1	.63	24.0	.02	.10	.01	.01	.07	.02	7.23	25.0	72.0	47.0	4.87	1.95	1.70	B	.25
	2	.63	22.0	.01	.08	.02	.01	.08	.01	7.15	24.0	71.0	47.0	4.78	2.90	1.80	B	.25
Elden Gatwood	1	.66	21.0	.01	.01	.01	.01	.01	.01	6.78	23.0	70.0	47.0	4.87	2.80	2.03	NS	.23
	2	.68	21.0	.01	.01	.01	.01	.01	.01	6.90	23.5	70.0	47.0	4.88	2.91	1.88	NS	.25
Fernand Gillet	1	.63	18.0	.05	.07	.02	.05	.05	.05	7.03	26.5	74.5	48.0	4.96	2.90	1.90	B	.28
	2	.61	17.0	.10	.13	.13	.13	.09	.10	7.06	27.0	75.0	48.0	4.89	2.85	1.70	B	.25
	3	.58	15.0	.10	.09	.08	.08	.08	.05	6.91	26.0	74.0	48.0	4.89	2.45	1.65	B	.28
Harold Gomberg	1	.63	22.0	.01	.02	.01	.04	.04	.01	7.25	25.0	70.0	45.0	4.78	3.00	1.75	B	.30
Ralph Gomberg	1	.56	23.0	.01	.05	.04	.01	.04	.01	7.25	25.5	72.5	47.0	4.95	2.80	1.70	B	.28
	2	.61	23.0	.01	.07	.08	.04	.05	.01	7.35	26.5	73.5	47.0	4.95	2.80	1.85	B	.25
Earnest Harrison	1	.63	21.0	.01	.05	.01	.01	.05	.01	7.00	26.0	71.5	46.0	4.69	2.75	1.65	NS	.25
	2	.61	18.0	.01	.04	.01	.01	.04	.01	7.22	23.5	70.5	47.0	4.92	2.85	1.75	NS	.28
Philip Kirchner	1	.61	17.0	.01	.04	.01	.01	.01	.01	7.05	24.5	72.0	48.0	4.85	2.80	1.75	B	.25
	2	.61	17.0	.02	.02	.01	.02	.04	.01	6.92	24.5	71.0	47.0	4.53	2.65	1.75	B	.20
Arthur Krilov	1	.58	20.0	.05	.10	.05	.05	.10	.05	7.18	24.0	72.0	47.0	4.80	2.90	1.70	B	.36
	2	.56	19.0	.02	.08	.05	.02	.05	.02	7.05	24.0	71.0	47.0	4.80	2.95	1.65	B	.28
Marc Lifschey	1	.61	15.0	.01	.01	.01	.01	.01	.01	6.95	26.5	72.5	46.0	4.87	2.55	1.80	NS	.30
	2	.61	14.0	.01	.01	.01	.01	.01	.01	6.85	25.0	72.0	47.0	4.82	2.80	1.85	B	.30

*Tip lost

TABLE 3 (*continued*)

Name	Reed No.	1 Center Thickness of Gouge	2 Length of Scrape	3 Tip Thickness Blade 1 (L C R)	3 Tip Thickness Blade 2 Opposing	4 Cane Width, Widest Point	5 Cane Length, Binding to Tip	6 Overall Length of Reed	7 Staple Length	8 Staple Dim. at Base, I.D.	9 Staple Dim. at Top, Long Axis of Ellipse, I.D.	10 Staple Dim. at Top, Short Axis of Ellipse, I.D.	11 Staple Material	12 Staple Material Thickness
UNITED STATES *continued*														
John Mack	1	.63	18.0	.01 .04 .01	.02 .04 .01	6.80	22.5	69.5	47.0	4.75	2.85	1.90	NS	.30
	2	.58	19.0	.01 .05 .01	.01 .04 .01	6.78	24.0	70.0	46.0	4.75	2.75	1.95	NS	.30
	3	.63	18.0	.01 .02 .01	.01 .02 .01	6.50	23.0	69.0	46.0	5.06	2.75	2.09	NS	.28
	4	.63	18.0	.01 .02 .01	.02 .02 .01	6.45	23.0	69.0	46.0	5.06	2.75	1.93	NS	.30
Arno Mariotti	1	.61	20.0	.01 .01 .01	.01 .01 .01	6.70	24.0	70.0	46.0	4.87	2.75	1.85	B	.28
	2	.63	20.0	.01 .01 .01	.01 .01 .01	6.82	24.0	70.5	46.5	4.94	2.75	1.85	B	.30
Philip Memoli, Jr.	1	.63	15.0	.02 .04 .05	.09 .08 .07	6.95	25.0	70.0	45.0	4.69	2.75	1.90	B	.33
	2	.63	15.0	.02 .05 .04	.04 .08 .04	7.00	26.0	70.0	44.0	4.81	2.80	1.80	B	.33
Florian Mueller	1	.63	15.0	.01 .01 .01	.01 .01 .01	6.85	22.0	70.0	43.0	4.71	2.85	1.75	B	.28
	2	.61	15.0	.01 .01 .01	.01 .01 .01	6.90	22.0	65.0	43.0	4.67	2.70	1.70	B	.25
Loyd Rathbun	1	.58	12.0	.01 .02 .02	.01 .02 .04	7.23	27.5	74.0	47.0	4.86	2.80	1.75	B	.28
	2	.58	13.0	.02 .07 .02	.01 .04 .01	7.15	27.0	73.5	47.0	4.87	2.80	1.80	B	.28
Merrill Remington	1	.56	13.0	.01 .01 .01	.01 .01 .01	7.00	25.0	71.0	46.0	4.87	2.70	1.75	B	.30
	2	.63	14.0	.01 .02 .01	.01 .02 .01	7.07	25.0	73.0	48.0	4.98	2.95	1.80	B	.30
	3	.61	14.0	.01 .01 .01	.01 .02 .01	7.25	25.5	72.0	47.0	4.87	2.90	1.65	B	.33
Paolo Renzi	1	.61	12.0	.01 .04 .01	.01 .04 .01	7.00	24.0	70.0	46.0	4.91	2.85	1.75	B	.30
	2	.61	11.0	.08 .05 .01	.02 .07 .02	7.00	23.0	70.0	47.0	4.78	3.00	1.65	B	.28
Joseph Rizzo	1	.61	11.0	.09 .13 .07	.05 .10 .05	6.55	27.0	74.0	47.0	4.79	2.60	2.00	B	.30
	2	.58	20.0	.02 .13 .02	.01 .13 .02	7.05	24.0	70.0	46.0	4.81	3.00	1.70	B	.28
Joseph Robinson	1	.63	20.0	.01 .02 .01	.01 .02 .01	6.73	23.0	70.0	47.0	4.87	2.98	1.99	NS	.30
	2	.63	19.5	.01 .02 .01	.01 .02 .01	6.82	21.5	68.5	47.0	4.87	2.90	2.01	NS	.33
Ronald Roseman	1	.61	20.0	.02 .08 .13	.02 .05 .02	7.15	24.0	70.5	47.0	4.88	2.89	1.78	NS	.25
	2	.61	19.0	.02 .02 .01	.02 .05 .13	6.95	24.0	70.5	47.0	4.86	2.99	2.01	NS	.25

Myron Russell	1	.63	17.0	.08	.08	.08	.13	.10	.08	7.00	26.0	72.5	47.0	4.99	2.90	2.10	B	.25
	2	.63	16.0	.04	.05	.04	.01	.04	.02	7.00	25.0	73.5	48.0	4.99	2.85	1.90	B	.28
Gordon Schoneberg	1	.66	24.0	.04	.04	.01	.02	.04	.05	6.87	24.0	71.0	47.0	4.77	2.90	1.75	B	.28
	2	.68	24.0	.02	.05	.05	.04	.08	.04	6.97	25.0	72.0	47.0	4.96	2.85	1.80	B	.25
Harry Shulman	1	.58	19.0	.01	.05	.01	.01	.05	.01	7.00	24.5	70.5	46.0	4.89	2.95	2.15	B	.30
	2	.58	19.0	.01	.05	.01	.01	.05	.01	7.02	24.5	70.5	46.0	4.90	2.90	2.10	B	.30
Robert Sprenkle	1	.56	17.0	.01	.01	.01	.01	.01	.01	6.77	24.0	70.0	46.0	4.75	2.55	1.80	B	.25
	2	.61	18.0	.01	.01	.01	.01	.01	.01	6.92	24.5	71.5	46.0	4.64	2.70	1.90	B	.28
Warren Stannard	1	.66	17.0	.01	.02	.01	.01	.02	.01	7.20	26.0	71.5	46.0	4.79	2.85	1.75	B	.30
	2	.68	17.0	.01	.02	.04	.01	.02	.05	7.25	26.0	71.0	46.0	4.90	2.75	1.85	B	.30
Ray Still	1	.58	21.0	.01	.02	.01	.01	.04	.01	7.05	23.0	68.0	45.0	4.83	2.80	1.90	B	.25
	2	.58	21.0	.02	.01	.04	.01	.01	.01	7.15	23.0	68.0	45.0	4.76	2.76	1.90	B	.30
Marcel Tabuteau	1	.56	17.0	.05	.08	.01	.04	.04	.02	7.10	28.0	76.0	47.0	4.90	2.75	2.00	B	.25
	2	.58	17.0	.01	.01	.01	.01	.01	.01	7.15	28.5	75.5	47.0	4.96	2.80	2.00	B	.28
	3	.53	22.0	.02	.05	.05	.05	.05	.02	6.82	22.0	68.5	47.0	4.86	2.83	1.90	NS	.33
	4	.56	19.0	.07	.08	.02	.10	.09	.04	7.11	21.0	67.5	47.0	4.82	2.80	1.96	NS	.30
Whitney Tustin	1	.63	15.0	.10	.10	.02	.05	.08	.05	6.85	25.0	71.0	46.0	5.01	2.65	2.00	B	.30
	2	.66	15.0	.07	.08	.07	.08	.08	.08	6.92	24.0	70.0	46.0	4.77	2.70	2.00	B	.28
Jean de Vergie	1	.61	15.0	.08	.08	.02	.09	.08	.02	7.00	25.5	72.0	47.0	4.86	2.85	1.75	B	.28
	2	.61	16.0	.11	.13	.07	.09	.15	.04	6.95	26.5	74.0	47.0	4.90	2.80	1.65	B	.25
	3	.63	15.0	.07	.07	.09	.08	.07	.07	6.90	26.0	73.5	47.0	4.87	2.85	1.65	B	.28
Raymond Weaver, Jr.	1	.66	17.0	.04	.04	.02	.04	.05	.02	6.95	24.5	70.0	46.0	4.87	2.65	1.80	B	.30
Richard Woodhams	1	.58	16.5	.01	.01	.01	.01	.01	.01	6.60	22.0	68.0	46.0	4.81	3.06	2.01	NS	.36
	2	.58	19.0	.01	.01	.01	.01	.01	.01	6.85	21.5	67.0	46.0	4.81	2.83	1.94	NS	.28

Table 4 is a frequency distribution chart of the *center thickness of the gouge* of the cane, to the nearest .oo mm., of the 168 examples (Table 3, column 1).

TABLE 4

Center Thickness of Gouge

A Frequency Distribution of Table 3, Column 1

Thickness in mm.	Distribution
.94	2
.81	2
.79	1
.76	2
.74	1
.71	1
.68	6
.66	6
.63	34
.61 (Median)	40
.58	34
.56	26
.53	8
.51	2
.48	1
.46	2
	168

The median (above and below which fall an equal number of cases) falls just eleven cases into the .61 millimeter thickness from the lower side. One hundred thirty-four cases, or 79.76 percent, fall between .56 millimeter and .63 millimeter. The Dutch examples are thickly gouged, obviously intentionally, showing that this feature is an important ingredient of the Dutch-style reed. Without these seven examples (.76 through .94 millimeter) the median would fall within four cases of the .58 millimeter (.023 inch) gouge thickness category. The writer considers this measurement one of the most important, possibly the most important, because the contour and thickness of the gouge dictates in large part the amount of cane removed proportionately from the different areas of the scrape in order to arrive at a particular sound, response, etc.

Table 5 is a frequency distribution chart of the *length of scrape* of the reeds (Table 3, column 2), to the nearest millimeter, except where the measurement was obviously .5 and could have been recorded as the millimeter either above or below.

TABLE 5

Length of Scrape
A Frequency Distribution of Table 3, Column 2

Length in mm.	Distribution
24	3
23	2
22	4
21	6
20	8
19	10
18	13 (Submedian)
17	12
16	11
15 (Median)	19
14	9
13	5
12	11
11	13
10	25 (Submedian)
9	14
8	2
7	1
	168

The median falls at 15 millimeters, above and below which there are clusters around two points, 10 millimeters and 18 millimeters. These two clusters statistically define the existence of the short-scrape and the long-scrape reed. For all practical purposes we find that a scrape shorter than 9 millimeters is rare indeed. (In fact it does not occur. The 7 millimeter example is the Barthel example, which has lost its tip over the years. One of the 8 millimeter examples is a Brierly that has also lost its tip, and the other example below 9 millimeters is the experimental Dandois, no.4, at 8 millimeters.) At the other extreme, the 24 millimeter examples are those of Gassman and Schoneberg.

Table 3, column 3, *Tip Thickness,* offers considerable material for observation. Even though it does not lend itself particularly well to tabular presentation and interpretation, the writer has analyzed column 3 to some degree in Tables 6A, B, C, and D. A great attempt was made to measure all the tips very carefully, in the same manner and in the same relative place on each blade. These tip measurements, in rare instances, include an element of judgment on the part of the writer, and in some absolutely necessary cases, an actual element of interpretation does exist. However, after several remeasurements it was found that although variations in the final individual measurements did occur at times, the *proportions* of the sides of the tip to the center and from one side to its opposing side almost invariably remained the same.

The dial indicator spring pressure (light) on the cane remained unchanged throughout all measurements, including the tip measurements. The cane was measured dry. Some slight, unintentional variation in measurement may have occurred because of the hardness or softness of certain pieces of cane, but in the writer's opinion, variation due to these factors was negligible.

The writer can visually detect a difference of approximately .04–.05 millimeter across a tip when holding it up to a light. It should be noted that the texture of the cane may hinder one's ability to detect these visible differences. A cane of very clear texture can mislead one into thinking that the tip is thinner than it actually is. This writer finds that a difference in thickness of .01 or .02 millimeter is extremely difficult, if not impossible, to detect with the unaided eye.

But, even though it may not be detectable visually, an actual physical difference of .01 or .02 millimeter in the thickness of the tip can make an appreciable difference in the playing characteristics of the reed. Just how much depends upon the comparative dimensions of other related factors existing in the reed as well as the thickness of the tip.

The writer believes that certain reedmakers perhaps have developed certain tendencies over their years of reedmaking experience. For example, there appears to be a conscious effort on the part of some reedmakers to make the thickness of both edges of the tip as nearly the same as possible. Others tend to leave the left side of the tip thicker than the right. This discrepancy between sides may be intentional, but it is more than likely attributable to the difficulty (for a right-handed person) of turning the knife around the left thumb. Allowing the plaque to extend too far to the left from between the blades of the reed also contributes to inequalities in thickness. The use of a narrower plaque will sometimes help solve this problem.

With relatively few exceptions, there seems to be a certain overall tendency for the center of the tips to be thicker than the sides. The writer does not know if this practice is an intentional one. The thickness in the center is probably caused by the fact that the cane is initially gouged thicker in the center. Also, as already noted, a difference of .01–.02 millimeter is very difficult to detect. In Table 3, column 3, one can note that some reedmakers tolerate tips that are quite unbalanced (diverse) in their tip measurements. No doubt the ill effects of such imbalance are absorbed, up to a point, in other areas of the reed.

The tips were measured at about .5 millimeter back from the left and right corners, and in the center, in order to get a useful, comparative measurement. On most reeds (depending upon the maker), if one measures a tip all the way across from corner to corner, one gets a different measurement at almost every point on the way across. Some of these differences are gradual and slight (.01 millimeter); others are quite abrupt, amounting to discrepancies as high as .02–.05 millimeter between points closer than $\frac{1}{16}''$.

Table 6A is a frequency distribution of all the *tip thickness measurements* in Table 3, column 3, *Blade 1 and Blade 2 combined.* The median of all the tip thickness measurements falls in the .02

TABLE 6A

Tip Thickness Measurements
*A Frequency Distribution of All Measurements
in Table 3, Column 3*

Thickness in mm.	Distribution
.01	380
.02 (Median)	182
.04	101
.05	137
.07	40
.08	89
.09	21
.10	27
.11	5
.13	14
.14	1
.15	5
.20*	4
.23*	2
	1008

From blades with lost tips

millimeter category. It is within 58 cases of the .01 category. This median, as usual throughout this study, is merely meant to be an indication of a central tendency—certainly not a suggestion that all reed tips should be .02 millimeter thick. As a matter of fact, the *greatest number of cases* falls in the .01 millimeter category, 79.4 percent of all the examples fall within the limits of .01 and .05 millimeter. The outside limits, beyond which there was no further tolerance in thickness, are .01 and .15 millimeter, plus or minus the round-off factors of .0061 and .0063 millimeter respectively. However, it is apparent that the majority of the observed examples have tips that are .02 millimeter thick or thinner, with the overall system able to absorb up to a very occasional .15 millimeter on a rather sharply declining curve.

Table 6B is a frequency distribution of the *variation of tip thickness* noted in *each reed* between Blade One and Blade Two at three opposite points: left corner (L), center (C), and right corner (R).

TABLE 6B

Variation of Tip Thickness Measurement,
Opposing Blades
From Table 3, Column 3

Variation in mm.	1. Opposing Corners, L Distribution	2. Opposing Centers, C Distribution	3. Opposing Corners, R Distribution
.00 (.0061 Possible)	93 (Median)	81	82
.01	25	24 (Median)	27 (Median)
.02	9	24	21
.03	29	23	24
.04	5	8	5
.05	2	6	2
.06	3	2	2
.07	1	0	2
.08	1	0	1
.11	0	0	1
.12	0	0	1
	168	168	168

1. The median variation between *opposing left corners* (the opposing left corner would be the right corner if the reed were viewed from the other side) falls in the .00 millimeter category, which could cause us to think that both sides were exactly the same and consequently well balanced indeed. Actually, variations of .00 up to .0061 millimeter are possible. Variations of .0063 millimeter and above were rounded-off into the next highest category (in this example—.01 millimeter). We note that a high 75.59 percent of the examples had a variation (toleration) of from .00 to .02 millimeter between opposing left corners, with the exceptions falling off sharply.

2. The median variation between *opposing center points* falls in the .01 millimeter category. However, more actual cases (81) prove that a variation of less than that was more desirable. (.0061 millimeter possible). A strong 76.78 percent of all the cases fall between .00 and .02 millimeter of variation between the thickness of center points of the blades at the tips.

3. The median variation between *opposing right corners* also

falls in the .01 millimeter category. But here again, the number of cases per category tells us that the smaller "up to .0061 millimeter variation" with 82 cases is more desirable than the larger .01 millimeter median category: there are almost three times the number of cases in the former group (82 versus 27).

Now, taking Table 6B as a whole, we can see that the outside limits of thickness variation between the three opposing points of the reed blades are .00 to .12 millimeter. But a toleration of even as much as .04 millimeter or more is extremely rare. It would seem that as little variation as possible, all other things being equal, would be most desirable. Perhaps one should strive for about .01 millimeter (half a thousandth of an inch).

Table 6C is a frequency distribution chart of the *greatest variation in tip thickness* measurements existing between the left, center, and right points (L, C, and R) *on each single blade* (168 reeds, 336 blades).

The median variation of thickness existing between the three points on a *single blade* falls in the .03 millimeter category. The

TABLE 6C

Variation of Tip Thickness Measurement,
Single Blades
From Table 3, Column 3

Variation in mm.	Distribution
.00 (.0061 Possible)	75
.01	54
.02	16
.03 (Median)	72
.04	39
.05	20
.06	26
.07	14
.08	8
.09	5
.10	1
.11	6
	336 Blades (168 Reeds)

highest number of cases (75) agree that .0061 millimeter variation can be tolerated between the three points. A high 82.14 percent of all of the examples tell us that .00 to .05 millimeter variation is tolerable. Greater variation would seem to best be considered *rare*.

Table 6D is a frequency distribution chart of the *greatest variation of tip thickness* that exists between *L, C,* and *R* on *both blades,* not just between any two given points on both blades or a single blade.

TABLE 6D

Variation of Tip Thickness Measurement,
Both Blades
From Table 2, Column 3

Variation in mm.	Distribution
.00 (.0061 Possible)	27
.01	17
.02	4
.03	35
.04 (Median)	20
.05	6
.06	20
.07	21
.08	7
.09	2
.10	1
.11	5
.12	3
	168

The median thickness variation between any two of the points (L, C, R) on *both* blades of the reed falls in the .04 millimeter category. Note that this is a greater variation (tolerance) than in Tables 6A, B, and C, obviously because of the greater difficulty in balancing the tips of two opposing blades (if indeed this was a goal of the reedmaker). 64.88 percent of the examples tell us that a variation of .00 to .05 millimeter in thickness is tolerable between both blades at the tip. The writer would consider as rare any varia-

tion beyond .07 millimeter. Note the 44 beautiful examples that
vary only .01 millimeter (half a thousandth of an inch) or less.

For practical application, the statistical analysis of tip thickness
measurements points up the fact that tips should be *thin* and *balanced* within rather clearly prescribed limits.

Table 7 is a frequency distribution of *cane width at the widest
point* of each reed; in other words, the greatest width of the shape.
There is a strong correlation between this measurement and the
largest width dimension of the shaper, even though in actual practice the dimension of the shaped cane usually turns out to be a
little smaller than the dimension of the metal pattern (shaper)
from which the cane is shaped.

The median falls in the 6.90 millimeter category. The middle 50
percent of all the cases lies between 6.80 millimeters and 7.10 millimeters.

All cases below 6.60 millimeters fall in the narrowest 10 percent.
All cases above 7.30 millimeters fall in the widest 10 percent.

The units containing the greatest number of cases each are 6.80,
6.85, 6.90, and 7.00 millimeters, with 19, 16, 13, and 16 cases, respectively

Stylistically, the Viennese reeds could be interpreted as wider
than medium; the German, on the average, narrower; the Dutch,
wider; and the Russian, wider. The English, French, and American
are medium width (with some exceptions, naturally).

We can note, for example, that most French-style reeds have a
width varying from 6.80 millimeters to 7.20 millimeters, approximately. Consequently, we would not expect to be able to make a
French-style reed that would be artistically and acoustically operable on present-day instruments with a cane width much beyond
these limits. This recommended range comprises approximately
.40 millimeters (half a millimeter or less), which may not seem to
be very much. But, as most reedmakers know, removing .05 millimeter or less from each side of a reed with a knife or fine emery
cloth will many times make an appreciable difference in the playing characteristics. On the other hand, the other proportions of a
reed may be such that even more must be taken from the width
before any real difference is noticed.

TABLE 7

Cane Width, Widest Point
A Frequency Distribution of Table 3, Column 4
(Rounded-off to nearest .05 mm.)

Width in mm.	Distribution
8.20	2
8.10	1
8.00	1
7.80	1
7.55	1
7.50	3
7.45	4
7.40	1
7.35	1
7.30	3
7.25	10
7.20	7
7.15	7
7.10	5
7.05	10
7.00	16
6.95 (Median)	9
6.90	13
6.85	16
6.80	19
6.75	10
6.70	4
6.65	4
6.60	8
6.55	5
6.50	4
6.40	1
6.15	1
6.10	1
	168

Table 8 is a frequency distribution chart of the *length of cane showing between the binding and the tip of the reed*. This measurement is an indication of the amount of potential vibrating mass

TABLE 8

Cane Length, Binding to Tip
A Frequency Distribution of Table 3, Column 5

Length in mm.	Distribution
28	7
27	15
26	27
25 (Median)	46
24	33
23	24
22	10
21	6
	168

of cane that is present. As we know, the art of reedmaking has to do with the removing of mass from certain areas of the blades in order to allow the remaining mass to vibrate in certain patterns. All other things being equal, this dimension *may* have the most influence on the pitch level of the reed.

The median length falls in the 25 millimeter category, or approximately 1 inch. The outside limits are 21 and 28 millimeters, but 77.38 percent of the reedmakers agree that there must be an even smaller range, 23 to 26 millimeters of cane above the binding.

This analysis brings to mind an explanation for the "extreme" examples of this and all the other tables. A reedmaker normally associates flatness of pitch with thick gouge; long length of scrape; wide shape; long cane length, binding to tip; long overall length; and long staple length (which can influence overall length). On the other hand, sharper pitch is associated with thinner gouge; shorter scrape; narrower shape; shorter cane length, binding to tip; shorter overall length; and shorter staple length.

In the balancing of all these dimensions, there is a good deal of potential for either strengthening or inhibiting a given playing characteristic. For example, the dimensions of the Parolari reeds in Table 3 would lead us to believe that the longer overall length (74 millimeters), longer cane length (27 millimeters), and wider shape (7.45 millimeters) would cause a low pitch level. This tendency is apparently compensated for by the shorter length of scrape (10 millimeters).

The Dandois examples provide another case in point: in these reeds the long overall length and long cane length are compensated for by the short scrape and a medium- to narrow-width shape.

Another example, indicative of the American style, comes from the reeds of Mack. Their measurements show a longer scrape (18 millimeters), which is compensated for by a narrower width of shape (6.80 and 6.50 millimeters), shorter cane length above the binding (22.5 and 23 millimeters), and a shorter overall length (69.5 and 69.0 millimeters).

A study of the Viennese reeds of Kamesch, Kautzky, and Raab and the Russian reed of Petrov will also show applications of the same principles. Actually, almost every reed in Table 3 can be analyzed in this way. If we note an abnormal dimension or set of dimensions, we can usually find a compensating dimension or set of dimensions. The long overall lengths (73 millimeters) of the Italians are compensated for (or necessitated by) the shorter scrape (10 millimeters). With Kalmus, extremely wide cane width (8.20 millimeters), and long cane length (27.5 millimeters) make it necessary for him to cut off the staple to 40 millimeters in order to play at an acceptable pitch level.

Clearly, there is no "correct" set of dimensions. Each style has its own acceptable limitations or it would not be a definable style. But within each of these styles, the individual player must arrive at his own "correct" dimensions.

At this point we can see that, just as there is a double reed of the Orient, there is a double reed in Western civilization, definable by a set of dimensional limitations into which fall all the styles we have discussed. We are documenting the living history of Western reedmaking, which will become the written history of the centuries to come. Within the context of the truism "the past is prologue," we can expect that in the centuries ahead, double reed dimensions will change as a result of different instrument specifications and new musical and aural demands.

Table 9 is a frequency distribution chart of *overall lengths* of the total number of examples.

The median falls almost in the center of the 71 millimeter dimension. Of the 168 cases, 13.09 percent are 74 millimeters and longer, 19.04 percent are 68 millimeters and shorter, and 63.09 percent are between 70 and 73 millimeters. The greatest number of cases falls in the 70 millimeter category. There are more extreme examples on the short side of the chart. Here again, this observation is a simple statement of fact and not meant to be a value judgment. As we have seen, there are ideological concepts and balancing characteristics that affect each dimension. However, the overall length has a great effect on the pitch level. Other proportions of the reed, acting upon each other and upon the total reed, affect such things as a balanced scale, tessitura, tone

TABLE 9

Overall Length of Reed
A Frequency Distribution of Table 3, Column 6

Length in mm.	Distribution
76	3
75	7
74	12
73	26
72 (Median)	28
71	23
70	29
69	8
68	12
67	5
66	1
65	5
64	1
63	2
62	3
61	1
59	1
58	1
	168

quality, response, etc. Consequently, when the reader studies column 6 or any of the other columns of Table 3, he should realize that a given dimension becomes meaningful only as it is related to another dimension, either on the same reed, a different reed, several reeds, or all reeds.

Table 10 is a frequency distribution of all *staple lengths*.

TABLE 10

Staple Length
A Frequency Distribution of Table 3, Column 7

Length in mm.	Distribution
49	4
48	21
47 (Median)	80
46	30
45	8
44	1
43	5
42	5
41	2
40	2
38	3
37	5
22	1
21	1
	168

The median falls at 47 millimeters, as does by far the greatest number of cases (80). If there is anything standardized about reed-making, perhaps it is the manufacture of staples to a certain length. In almost every case where a staple is shorter than 47 millimeters, it is noticeable that it has been cut off at the large end.

There are many more examples of staples shorter than 47 millimeters than there are of those longer than that. The writer surmises that it has been found necessary to shorten the staple in order to balance (raise) the pitch level. The length of the staple, of course, affects the overall length of the reed.

TABLE 11

Staple Dimension at Base, Inside Diameter
A Frequency Distribution of Table 3, Column 8
(Rounded-off to nearest .05 mm.)

Diameter in mm.	Distribution
5.10	1
5.05	3
5.00	9
4.95	15
4.90	27
4.85 (Median)	37
4.80	29
4.75	14
4.70	8
4.65	15
4.60	1
4.55	4
4.50	1
4.45	2
4.35	8
	168

Table 11 is a frequency distribution chart of the *dimension of the inside diameter of the circular base of the staple.*

The median falls in the 4.85 millimeter unit, which also contains the greatest number of cases (37). The number of categories on the narrower side of the median is almost twice that on the wider side. The narrower measurements are due in slight part to cutting off the staple. Also, it is obvious upon examination that some staples were initially manufactured smaller.

With only 37 cases in the largest category, it is apparent that there is no industry standard. Or, if there is, these staples have undergone a selection process by the player to fit with a number of other characteristics such as instrument bore, gouge of cane, etc., so that a "good reed" can be made. Indeed, certain staples *do* seem to be better than others and better reeds are made on those staples time after time.

On the other hand, it also appears that in this dimension a variation of .10 millimeter does not make a great deal of difference, except past a critical point, that point being the correct amount of mismatching with the bore of the player's oboe.

The writer had a set of seven staples made, the smallest of which (no. 1) was three graduated units *smaller* than the bore of his oboe. No. 4 was the *same* size as the bore so that the staple was a smooth continuation of the bore, and no. 7 was three graduated units *larger* than the bore. After repeated testing with Lorée BD 5 and Lorée BO 40, the writer found that he prefers a slightly increasing step between the upper bore of the instrument and the staple, which is preferably of slightly larger inside diameter than the bore of the oboe.

On both these instruments, the small ends of the bores, where they meet the staple, are very close to the same diameter: BD 5 measures 4.85 millimeters, and BO 40 measures 4.87 millimeters, a difference so slight as to be negligible. A slight bit of miscalculation of "feel" of the measuring instrument may easily account for a deviation of .01 or .02 millimeter. Coincidentally, the writer's Lorée bores match the 4.85 millimeter mean diameter of the large end (base) of the staples surveyed in this study.

There is quite a lot of deviation among oboe-bore measurements, but certainly not as much as in staples. One need only measure a few to see for himself how uneven the inside diameters of staples really are. Perhaps this situation is good for the selection process, for if the staples were too exact there would be less chance for flexibility. All lapped staples tend to be fairly rough in their measurements, no doubt because of the method of manufacture. Of all the staples surveyed the one of Tait bears a unique distinction. It has the most accurate, smooth inside diameter of all. Certainly the fact that it is made by electrodeposition contributes to this beautiful accuracy.

Table 12 is a frequency distribution of the *dimension of the staple* at the *small end* (top) across the *wide inside diameter* of the oval.

The median width falls in the 2.80 millimeter category and the greatest number of cases also falls in this category (33). Seventy percent fall between 2.70 and 2.90 millimeters. The distance be-

TABLE 12

Staple Dimension at Top, Long Axis of Ellipse,
Inside Diameter
A Frequency Distribution of Table 3, Column 9
(Rounded-off to nearest .05 mm.)

Width in mm.	Distribution
3.80	1
3.50	1
3.10	2
3.05	1
3.00	6
2.95	6
2.90	20
2.85	26
2.80 (Median)	33
2.75	17
2.70	22
2.65	9
2.60	10
2.55	6
2.50	4
2.45	1
2.30	1
1.95	1
1.85	1
	168

tween the outside limits is just short of 2 millimeters. Table 12 gains its greatest significance when compared with Table 13.

Table 13 is a frequency distribution of the *dimension of the staple* at the *small end* across the *short inside diameter* of the oval.

The median (84) falls in the 1.90 millimeter category as does the greatest number of cases (30).

The measurements of Table 3, columns 9 and 10, help to determine the shape of the oval end of the staple. Only one example was truly circular, that of the Leningrad Symphony player (2.50–2.50 millimeters). Petrov no. 1 (1.85–1.65 millimeters), Gassman no. 1 (1.95–1.70 millimeters), and Tait (3.50–3.05 millimeters) approach being circular.

TABLE 13

Staple Dimension at Top, Short Axis of Ellipse,
Inside Diameter
A Frequency Distribution of Table 3, Column 10
(*Rounded-off to nearest .05 mm.*)

Width in mm.	Distribution
3.05	1
2.50	1
2.20	5
2.15	7
2.10	13
2.05	6
2.00	16
1.95	18
1.90 (Median)	30
1.85	15
1.80	20
1.75	15
1.70	11
1.65	8
1.50	2
	168

The reader can estimate the approximate shape of the small opening by noting the difference between the wide and narrow measurements. A difference of .15–.50 millimeter gives a rather fat oval; Baker's no. 2, 1.85–3.80 millimeters, is a very flat oval.

The four preceding staple measurements (the length and the three opening measurements, Table 3, columns 7, 8, 9, and 10) determine the taper of the staple and thereby have an influence on the opening of the reed. However, a more important factor that influences the opening of the reed is the tube from which the cane was cut.

The famous words "this staple must be correct—it fits my mandrel" cannot be true unless the mandrel is correct for the instrument and the player. Even then, the gross measurements and interior irregularities and distortions of staples make it difficult to determine that the staple does in fact fit the mandrel.

Table 3, column 11, is a simple notation of the *material from which the staple was made.* Thirty-two were nickel silver and 136 were brass.

Table 14 is a frequency distribution of the *thickness of the staple material.* These are average figures because of the great variations in thickness.

TABLE 14

Staple Material Thickness
A Frequency Distribution of Table 3, Column 12

Thickness in mm	Distribution
.43	1
.41	1
.38	5
.36	11
.33	12
.30	51
.28 (Median)	49
.25	23
.23	8
.20	6
.18	1
	168

The median falls exactly in the .28 millimeter category, and the greatest numbers of cases are in the .30 millimeter category. It is not uncommon to find a variation of .05 millimeter or more in the thickness of the material of any given staple. This tendency is particularly likely when the inside is pitted at the seam. But the deviation is not limited to that condition.

The writer does not suggest that a reed made to the average dimensions of the foregoing tables would necessarily be a "good" reed. We have seen that many factors may have an effect upon the final dimensions of a reed that is capable of being played artistically by a given player. However, it is at least interesting to note the following rounded average figures in millimeters.

Gouged cane	.61 (.024″)
length of scrape	14.55
short scrape	10.60
long scrape	17.75
Average tip thickness	.03
variation, opposing left corners	.0149
variation, opposing centers	.0157
variation, opposing right corners	.0165
variation, single blade	.0247
variation, both blades	.0373
Width of shape at widest point	6.88
Cane length, binding to tip	24.82
Overall length	69.51
Staple length	45.44
base, i.d.	4.79
long axis, small end, i.d.	2.77
short axis, small end, i.d.	1.90
material	Brass
thickness of material	.28

The foregoing reed survey gives a considerable, objective view of the possibilities and limitations practiced in contemporary oboe reedmaking in the Western world. The oboist has at his disposal approximately five basic scrapes (styles) of reeds within a variable spectrum. At one extreme of the spectrum there is a dark, thick, tone quality; at the other extreme, a bright, nasal timbre. The five scrapes (styles) are merely discernible areas (clusters of examples with like characteristics) on a scale of an infinite number of differences. Because of the player's aural conception, instrument, em-

bouchure, playing environment, or teacher, it is possible, and perhaps desirable, to combine certain characteristics of different
schools or to modify one particular method toward one side or the
other of the spectrum. This objective may be achieved by varying
the measurements of scrape, gouge, width of shape, etc.

Of course, it would be impossible for a student to study with all
the players represented in this volume. This study then also gives
the student a visual and dimensional representation of the style of
reed that these artists make (or made) and, consequently, gives
some indication of the sound characteristics of the various styles.
How and *why* does an oboist sound the way he does? The cut of
the reed is one of the answers.

It is true that one can only guess at how a reed will sound simply
by looking at it. Possibly, it will not vibrate at all. The visual representations are a valid indication of a sound characteristic only if
many comparisons are involved. We learn, through practice and
judgment, to expect the results of certain dimensions *and* altered
dimensions. Many of the dimensions and alterations are visually
obvious.

One must remember that all the factors of playing the oboe
(method of breathing, embouchure, instrument, playing situation,
etc.) are interrelated. If one factor varies, it can effect a change in
another factor or other factors.

So, in summary, the styles of reedmaking are synonymous with
the methods and measurements of reedmaking and have evolved
primarily for two reasons. The *first* one is that the artist-player
has the desire to produce a certain timbre, born of a personal aural
concept, sometimes influenced by the listener. Timbre has certain
technical aspects or properties that influence the cut and dimensions of the reed, and these properties can be modified by modify-
ing the reed, within limits, to suit the aural concept of the player.
Usually the player is influenced by the listener, in that he wishes
his playing to be sociologically accepted. The *second* factor that
makes a delineation of reed styles possible is that the player desires,
indeed, is faced with the necessity for, a technique adequate
enough to express himself musically, according to his musical taste.
This technique is dependent, in part, upon the cut, dimensions, and
timbre of the reed. The technical aspects of the factors involved

in tone production and their pedagogical implications have been discussed in chapters 2 through 7.

Now, to return to the basic proposition in chapter 1, each style of oboe reed represents a compromise in a number of variable dimensions that permit the player to control, within certain limits, the timbre, pitch, dynamics, and articulation. By a realistic appraisal of the various styles of reeds and their respective possibilities for tone and control, we have seen that it is possible for a player to exercise an intelligent selection and adjustment of his reed and thus improve his performing ability.

Most players, understandably, do not know the overall possibilities and limitations inherent in reedmaking. They have in many instances attempted and succeeded, through trial and error, to arrive at a properly balanced method of playing for their purposes. Through the preceding analysis the writer hopes to make available to students and professionals more of the possibilities involved in reedmaking and their relation to oboe playing. May your quest for your perfect reed be a happy one.

NOTES

INTRODUCTION

1. *Schwann Long Playing Record Catalogue.* W. Schwann, Inc., 137 Newbury Street, Boston, Massachusetts, 02116. Also see "Baroque Music for Oboe—A Discography," by Daniel Stolper with Virginia Lowrey in *The Journal of the International Double Reed Society*, no. 2, 1974.

CHAPTER ONE: RESPIRATION

1. The source for this section on muscles is *Morris' Human Anatomy* (Philadelphia: P. Blakeston's Son and Co., 1923).

2. For a discussion of the factors that affect the resistance of the reed, see Robert Sprenkle and David Ledet, *The Art of Oboe Playing* (Evanston, Illinois: Summy-Birchard Company, 1961).

CHAPTER FOUR: THE INSTRUMENT

1. For photographs of *surna* and reed, see Plate XVIII in Anthony Baines, *Woodwind Instruments and Their History* (New York: W. W. Norton and Co., 1957). For one discussion of this migration see Arthur Bridet, *L'education du Hautboiste* (Paris: Aux Editions de la Pensée Latine, 1928).

2. Joseph Marx, "The Tone of the Baroque Oboe," *The Galpin Society Journal*, no. 4 (June 1951): 3.

3. For photographs, see Plate II, no. 2 in Phillip Bate, *The Oboe* (New York: Philosophical Library, 1956). Also see Plate XXIII, no. 4, and fig. 63, no. 4, in Baines, *Woodwind Instruments*, p. 170.

4. Anthony Baines, "Shawms of the Sardana Coblas," *The Galpin Society Journal*, no. 5 (March 1952): 9. Charles McNett, "The Chirimia: A Latin American Shawm," *The Galpin Society Journal*, no. 13 (July 1960): 44.

5. For photograph, see Plate II, no. 4, in Bate, *The Oboe*. Also see Plate II, B, in Éric Halfpenny, "The French Hautboy: A Technical Survey," *The Galpin Society Journal*, no. 6 (July 1953): 23. A picture of the true oboe appears in the earliest known French tutor for oboe, Freillon Poncein's *La Veritable Maniere d'Apprendre a Jouer . . . du Hautbois* (Paris: J. Colombat, 1700), copies of which exist at the Library of Congress and at the Paris Conservatoire.

6. Marx, "The Tone of the Baroque Oboe."

7. Bate, *The Oboe*, p. 35.

8. Marx, "The Tone of the Baroque Oboe."

9. This point is well discussed in Baines, *Woodwind Instruments*, p. 277, and Bate, *The Oboe*, p. 34.

10. Baines, *Woodwind Instruments*, p. 278.

11. Anthony Baines, "James Talbot's Manuscript," *The Galpin Society Journal*, no. 1 (March 1948): 9; Baines, *Woodwind Instruments*, p. 278; Halfpenny, "The French Hautboy"; Thomas Warner, "Two Late Eighteenth-Century Instructions for Making Double Reeds," *The Galpin Society Journal*, no. 15 (March 1962): 27.

12. Halfpenny, "The French Hautboy."

13. Eric Halfpenny, "The English 2- and 3-Keyed Hautboy," *The Galpin Society Journal*, no. 2 (March 1949): 10.

14. See Plates II, III, IV, and V in Bate's *The Oboe* for excellent photographs of the transition from shawm to pre-1700 true oboe, on through the eighteenth-century classical oboe, and thence through the stages of development of the nineteenth-century oboe. Plate I shows photographs of modern oboes. Other photographs of modern oboes appear in Plate VIII in Baines, *Woodwind Instruments*.

15. Baines, *Woodwind Instruments*, p. 281.

16. Warner, "Two Late Eighteenth-Century Instructions."

17. See fig. 9, p. 62, in Bate, *The Oboe*.

18. For photographs, see fig. 13, p. 86, and Plate IV, no. 6 (Zuleger) in Bate, *The Oboe*. Also see Plate IX, nos. 3 and 4, in Baines, *Woodwind Instruments*.

19. James A. MacGillivray, "Woodwind and Other Orchestral Instruments in Russia Today," *The Galpin Society Journal*, no. 10 (May 1957): 3.

20. After Harry F. Olson, *Musical Engineering* (New York: McGraw-Hill Book Co., 1952).

21. The writer uses "partials" as distinct from "overtones" or "harmonics." The fundamental is the first partial; the octave is the second partial; the twelfth is the third partial; etc. The fundamental has no "overtone" or "harmonic" counterpart. The octave is the first overtone or harmonic; the twelfth is the second overtone or harmonic; and so on.

| Fundamental | 1st partial | |
| Octave | 2nd partial | 1st overtone or harmonic |

12th	3rd partial	2nd overtone or harmonic
15th	4th partial	3rd overtone or harmonic
etc.	etc.	etc.

22. A short explanation of this theorem for our purposes (certainly an oversimplification from the physicist's viewpoint) is to say that as air (or liquid) velocity increases, pressure decreases. Let us take the case of the airplane wing as an example. The air molecules rushing with greater velocity over the curved topside of the wing cause a comparative drop in pressure on the topside of the wing. This allows the relative increase in pressure from below to push into the area of low pressure above, thereby causing "lift."

23. The clarinet is not a "truly" stopped pipe because it does produce a few very weak even-numbered partials.

CHAPTER FIVE: THE ACOUSTICS OF THE ROOM

1. See W. T. Bartholomew, *Acoustics of Music* (New York: Prentice-Hall, 1942), pp. 64–65.

CHAPTER SEVEN: REEDS OF INDIVIDUAL OBOISTS

1. Harry Shulman, "Guide to a Flexible Oboe: The Problem of Dark versus Bright Tone," in *The Woodwind Anthology* (1952), pp. 57–58.
2. Whitney Tustin, "An Oboe Reed a Day," *Woodwind Magazine* (March 1951).

CHAPTER EIGHT: A DELINEATION OF REED STYLES

1. See photographs of early reeds in Anthony Baines, *Woodwind Instruments And Their History* (New York: W. W. Norton and Co., 1957). Also see drawings and descriptions of reeds in early tutors and the excellent articles by Halfpenny in *The Galpin Society Journal.*
2. For a discussion of oboe designs and styles, including the Zuleger oboe, see Baines, *Woodwind Instruments,* pp. 92–95. See Philip Bate, *The Oboe* (New York: Philosophical Library, 1956), pp. 74–75, 85–87, for a discussion of the German-type oboe.
3. See Baines, *Woodwind Instruments,* Plate VI, no. 7; Plate XIX, nos. 5 and 6; and Plate XXII.
4. It is interesting to note that when one compares the two predominate scrapes of reed—the short and the long—the short scrape must necessarily have a longer lay (less thickness in the heart, or, in other words, the heart placed further back from the tip). This is necessary in order to allow the reed to vibrate adequately because no rind is scraped from the back of the reed. On the long-scrape reed the heart can be left thicker, as blowing resistance is lowered by removing rind from the back. Short-scrape reeds tend to be "brighter" in sound; long-scrape reeds tend to be "darker" in sound. Mid-range scrapes vary the principle proportionately.

BIBLIOGRAPHY

Backus, John. *The Acoustical Foundations of Music.* New York: W. W. Norton, Inc., 1977.

Baines, Anthony. "James Talbot's Manuscript." *The Galpin Society Journal,* no. 11 (March 1948): 9.

———. "Shawms of the Sardana Coblas." *The Galpin Society Journal,* no. 5 (March 1952): 9.

———. *Woodwind Instruments and Their History.* New York: W. W. Norton and Co., 1957.

Bate, Phillip. *The Oboe.* New York: Philosophical Library, 1956.

Bartholomew, W. T. *Acoustics of Music.* New York: Prentice-Hall, Inc., 1942.

Bhosys, Waldemar. "The Reed Problem." In *The Woodwind Anthology* (1952), pp. 58–60.

———. "Oboe Reed Standardization." In *The Woodwind Anthology* (1952), pp. 58–60.

Evans, Kenneth G. "Instructional Materials for the Oboe, 1695–ca. 1800." Ph.D. dissertation, State University of Iowa, 1963.

Gomberg, Harold. "On Oboe Cane." *Woodwind World,* II (February 1958).

Goossens, Leon, and Roxburgh, Edwin. *Oboe.* New York: Schirmer Books, 1977.

Halfpenny, Eric. "The English 2- and 3-Keyed Hautboy." *The Galpin Society Journal,* no. 2 (March 1949): 10.

———. "The French Hautboy: A Technical Survey," Part I. *The Galpin Society Journal,* no. 6 (July 1953): 23.

———. "The French Hautboy: A Technical Survey," Part II. *The Galpin Society Journal,* no. 8 (March 1955): 50.

Jeans, Sir James. *Science and Music.* New York: Macmillan, 1928.

McAninch, Daniel A. "Technical Problems of the Oboe in the Woodwind Quintet." Ph.D. dissertation, Eastman School of Music, 1956.

MacGillivray, James A. "Woodwind and Other Orchestral Instruments in Russia Today." *The Galpin Society Journal,* no. 10 (May 1957): 3.

McNett, Charles. "The Chirimia: A Latin American Shawm." *The Galpin Society Journal*, no. 13 (July 1960): 44.

Marx, Joseph. "The Tone of the Baroque Oboe." *The Galpin Society Journal*, no. 4 (June 1951): 3.

Morris' Human Anatomy. Philadelphia: P. Blakeston's Son and Co., 1923.

Olson, Harry F. *Musical Engineering*. New York: McGraw-Hill Book Co., 1952.

Pardue, Robert E. "Arundo donax–Source of Musical Reeds and Industrial Cellulose," *Economic Botany*, XII (October–December 1958): 368–404.

Russell, Myron Edward. "The Oboe–A Comparison Study of Specifications with Musical Effectiveness." Ph.D. dissertation, University of Michigan, 1953.

Seashore, G. E. *The Psychology of Musical Talent*. New York: Silver, Burdett and Co., 1919.

Shulman, Harry. "Guide to a Flexible Oboe, the Problem of Dark versus Bright Tone." In *The Woodwind Anthology* (1952), pp. 57–58.

Sprenkle, Robert, and Ledet, David. *The Art of Oboe Playing*. Evanston, Illinois: Summy-Birchard Company, 1961.

Storch, Ben. "Exploding the Oboe Myth." In *The Woodwind Anthology* (1952), pp. 11–12.

Tustin, Whitney. "An Oboe Reed a Day." *Woodwind Magazine* (March 1951).

Warner, Thomas. "Two Late Eighteenth-Century Instructions for Making Double Reeds." *The Galpin Society Journal*, no. 15 (March 1962): 27.

Davɪᴅ A. Lᴇᴅᴇᴛ, Professor Emeritus of Music at the University of Georgia, is co-author of *The Art of Oboe Playing*.

CPSIA information can be obtained
at www.ICGtesting.com
Printed in the USA
BVHW01s1501201217
503317BV00002B/204/P